1994

Love, Edie

D1250889

OPStime

OPStime

THE SECRET TO PERFECT TIMING FOR SUCCESS

By Robert Taylor

LONGSTREET PRESS
Atlanta, Georgia

Published by
LONGSTREET PRESS, INC.
A subsidiary of Cox Newspapers,
A division of Cox Enterprises, Inc.
2140 Newmarket Parkway
Suite 118
Marietta, GA 30067

Copyright © 1994 by Robert D. Taylor

All rights reserved. No part of this book may be reproduced in any form or by any means without the prior written permission of the Publisher, excepting brief quotations used in connection with reviews, written specifically for inclusion in a magazine or newspaper.

OPStime™, Optimum Performance Schedule™ and OPS™ are registered trademarks of Optimum Performance Technologies.

Printed in the United States of America

1st printing 1994

ISBN 1-56352-187-3

This book was printed by Arcata Graphics, Kingsport, Tennessee.

Book design and production by Graham & Company Graphics.
Jacket design by Laura McDonald.

For

the faith in discovering and to those who believe in and
assist the discoverer

With thanks to

Lynn McGill, for without her this book would not be;
Marjorie, my daughter whose enthusiasm spurred me on;
David, my son, who exercised my physical soul after hours;
Harry, the filling station of knowledge, belief and wisdom;
Wendy, Tony, Cindi and Tim for holding down the fort;
Robyn Spizman and Dr. Marianne Garber, Ph.D.,
for their continuing inspiration and wisdom;

and especially

Miss Carrie
my beloved wife

Table of Contents

Foreword **xi**

Introduction: The Rhythm of the Day **1**

OPStime: Age-old Secrets Revealed 1
Hundreds of Clocks 3
Thoughts to Actions 6

1 OPStime **7**

Charting Peak Performance Times 7
The Search 8
The Final Key 13
The Formula for Success 14
Questions and Answers 15
The Breakthrough 17

2 The Optimum Performance Schedule **19**

How to Know When 19
Secrets Revealed 20
Understanding the Schedule 21
Color and Productivity 22
What's Hot, What's Not 26

3 **On Time Sales** 31

From the Second Floor, Straight Up 32
Change, Adapt and Care 33
The Old and the New 34
Validating Results 35
OPS Strategies for Better Sales 39
There's a Wrong Time for Everything 41
Questions and Answers 43

4 **Managing On Time** 47

Best Strategy Analysis 49
Managing a Restaurant 50
A Director of Human Resources 55
Questions and Answers 60

5 **Marketing, Advertising and Public Relations** 63

OPS: Taylor's Marketing Advantage 65
The Many Hats of Lewis Kinney 68
Ad Energy Marketing Group 72
Public Relations Challenges 76

6 **What's OPS, Doc?** 83

Medicine and Psychiatry Come in on Time 83
Time for Medicine 85
Babies 86
Premenstrual Syndrome 88
Anesthesia 90

Cancer 90
Heart Disease 92
Mental OPS and Downs 93
Seasonal Affective Disorder 94
Depression 96
Stress 99
Sleep Disorders 100
Eating Disorders 102
OPS and Elder Care 105

7 **Personal Best** **107**

The OPS Personal Profile: It's You! 107
A Senior Real Estate Investment Analyst 108
A Second-Shift Quality Control Inspector 113
A Singer/Songwriter 115
Personality Style and OPS 118

8 **A Magic Carpet Ride** **127**

The Future Runs by the OPS 127
Back into Time 127
The World According to OPS 128
Accidents 129
A Spot for Sports 131
In and Out of Time 132
OPS in My Job Description 134
OPS . . . Your Life and Style 136
As Good as Gold 137
Just in Case 138

Foreword

Dear Reader,

I have been a businessman all my life and have enjoyed a good deal of success. From its beginnings in 1969, I have built my company to the largest of its kind in the Southeast and become a multimillionaire in the process.

Like any successful businessman, I constantly strive to find an edge that will improve sales. My search has taken me down fascinating roads, where I have hunted the proverbial "better mousetrap." Surprisingly enough, one of those trips led me not to a new discovery, but to an age-old secret that became my road map to success. With this knowledge, I created a system that gives me an edge every day in each endeavor I undertake. With it, I have enhanced my company's sales by 25 percent per annum over our previous averages and learned how to increase my personal success manyfold.

In this book, you will learn the secret of the system I now call OPS—Optimum Performance Schedule—and how to use it to maximize your success in everything you do. However, do not assume this is another how-to book on profitability, management or sales. This is a when-to book.

You already know how to achieve. You already know what your goals are. What I am going to share with you is when to put your know-how to work. OPS can show you what time of day you can increase your chances of victory in each endeavor. Every day.

Am I saying I can predict the future? No, because I know something more critical to success. The future is mine because I know how and when to act. With the schedule in this book, you can too—in advance. This when-to technology offers you the opportunity of a lifetime.

Why am I sharing this miraculous secret with you? Why not? I won't be any less successful because you have the secret and can achieve your personal goals more easily. I genuinely hope that soon you too can participate in the prosperity and happiness I have come to experience.

Sincerely,

Robert David Taylor

Robert David Taylor

OPStime

INTRODUCTION

THE RHYTHM OF THE DAY

OPStime: Age-old Secrets Revealed

Salesmen are always hyping their products as "something new under the sun," a "better mousetrap," a "new pet rock" and a "pot of gold" all rolled into one. What I'm going to share with you in this book has its roots in history. A very long history—human behavioral patterns. Applied in an innovative and purposeful way, this knowledge could change your life. It's changed mine and my company's. I have a story to tell you that will change the way you plan your day, book your appointments and make your investment decisions. What I want to share with you is the *real* secret to productivity. That may sound incredible, but it's the truth.

I've been in business since 1969. For many of those years I was in sales. Even today, as CEO of several companies, I value my sales experience and lead my sales forces with principles I picked up at this early stage.

Many times over the years, I noticed that I had good times and bad times. Sometimes I could do no wrong. Other times I could do no right. You've probably felt the same way. Curiously, my salespeople appeared to do the same thing, together as well as individually. Coincidence? I wondered.

Why is it that given nearly an identical set of circumstances, outcome varies so widely? At this point, many people shrug their shoulders, blame it on sun spots, the wrong side of the bed, or the weather. But not me. Beyond the schedule dictated by the workday, I figured another kind of order must be influencing behavior.

Sometimes my employees were "on"; other times the whole place seemed switched "off." They all knew *how* to do their jobs, but *when* to do certain things eluded them. My sales force would, for example, have a great morning and a lousy afternoon and maybe some middling times in between. I could not decide if they were responding to trends in buying and selling habits, perhaps seasonal, or responding to something else. Even parties appeared to rise and fall by some signal, as though a remote control were being pointed at the crowd, changing the channel and the mood of the event. But there was no readily evident pattern.

At a local mall one afternoon, I was walking through a store on my way back to my car after a quick lunch when I noticed a tie and decided to purchase it immediately. Even after lunch, the mall was still crowded, and in many stores long lines formed in front of busy cash registers. "I wonder why everybody comes at once," muttered a salesperson from whom I was buying the tie. "Probably the same reason my sales force is out there selling up a storm," I replied.

Little did I realize the truth of that statement.

For a long time, I simply observed people. My observations convinced me again and again that some internal cues were impacting the way people both acted upon and responded to events. Then one evening while studying some books on magnetic fields, a recollection of something called *circadian rhythms* poked out of a recess in my memory. It occurred to me that these rhythms might affect the behavior I was seeing all around me. Reaching back into the dimness of college biology classes, I recalled the biological clocks that regulate all animals, plants and people, and that don't follow the artificial timing of the strict 24-hour solar/lunar day. "Maybe that's what is ticking," I thought.

I think all the events of my life conspired to produce this vision. Even my boyhood, spent sailing on the lakes in Michigan, inspired my continuing love of the outdoors. At every opportunity I take my family to a vacation spot where we can ski, fish or hike. My adventures in the natural world made me sensitive to being without a watch, forcing me to depend on biological clocks for my activities.

For many years I thought "vacation schedules" had nothing to do with that "Monday Morning Effect" that many of us experience upon returning to work. Then, one day in the mid-1980s, I attended a conference at the office of a major building materials distributor. A number of us were sitting in an informal meeting talking about cycles: cycles of financing, clusters of sales, cycles of cancellations, cycles of cash sales, cycles of financed sales. People were talking about ways to figure out the cycles in advance, speculating on their causes. Many of the people—business leaders from all over the country—attached great significance to seasons. That covered a few things, but certainly didn't begin to be the basis for every item under discussion.

That evening was the beginning. I became convinced that something out there was coordinating with cyclical data. I thought that if I could figure out what that "something" was, patterns might be predictable. And if I could predict them, productivity in my company would skyrocket.

Hundreds of Clocks

Beginning my search, I delved into studies about circadian rhythms. The more I read, the more I became convinced that these biological rhythms were influencing both my own behavior and that of the people around me.

I found that researchers in a field developed during the 1960s called *chronobiology* were intensely studying biological clocks, and had found hundreds of separate biological timing mechanisms. For my purposes, there were three types of clocks involved in what I was trying to discover.

Ultradian clocks measure time units less than a day in length; *infradian* clocks keep big cycles moving—menses, pregnancy, life cycles. Both of these are like little clocks hung on the walls of each cell in every body. They govern inner time, and are dependent upon the individual. *Circadian* clocks, the ones scientists actually know the most about, operate independently of the individual person, yet influence the body's overall timekeeping. They are based on a "day" approximately 25 hours long. All of these internal clocks are precision instruments, delicately balanced and essential to life. They command a system of intricate interrelatedness. My purpose, as it developed, was to find out how the circadian clocks impacted life as we live it.

I could see empirical results of something moving through solar/lunar time, but I still could not find the key to the apparently illogical pattern. Doing what I knew best, I set about cataloging times, particularly when sales seemed up or down. I wanted to create a system by which I could predict *when* good sales would most likely be made.

But that turned out to be only the beginning.

I began wanting to know what the rhythms meant to modern-day society. What impact did they have on our daily lives? We believe that in our sophistication we have abstracted ourselves with sidewalks and steel from these rhythms. We think that a 24-hour day and an eight-hour work schedule remove us from our biological clocks which can be automatically reset when the sun comes up.

But once I learned how, connecting to other kinds of time became simple, and so many of the things people do began to make incredible sense to me. For example, my wife and I backpack in the mountains, often for days at a time. Life there returns quickly to the circadian rhythms that regulate the behavior of all living things. When we remove our wristwatches, and with them our artificial 24-hour structure, we eat and sleep *with* the flow of time rather than against it. I'm sure you have felt these same rhythms on vacations to the beach or the mountains. But back at work or school, our 24-hour day looms large in our scheduling. What I began to discover, however, was that no amount of resetting of our internal clocks could dim the beat of those natural rhythms.

I began to get excited about the possibilities. Why would our internal clocks reset at sunrise? What time was I *really* on that they would need resetting? Tuned into an idea that daily became less abstract and more concrete, I started to notice my own sleep patterns. Have you ever awakened after four hours of sleep completely refreshed and after ten feeling like a lead balloon? I have, and when I stopped blaming the weather, work or family for these things, I was able to listen to the internal ticking of my biological clocks—and to the push and pull of the circadian rhythms.

At my office each day, I noted the times of what I could only describe as the "mood" of the employees across the board. Up times and down times seemed as though they were shared throughout the company. Tuned in as I was to the biological clocks, these patterns started making sense to me.

One day I came across the book *How to Feel Great 24 Hours a Day* (Simon and Shuster, New York, 1983) by the great author/lecturer/athlete/cardiologist Dr. George Sheehan. He talks about circadian rhythms, convinced that we pay too little attention to them. "These tides within the body are too important to be used simply for the delight of the mind. They must be lived. They must be acted out so that each of us gets the most out of the bodies we inhabit," he says.

What Dr. Sheehan, as well as others, including the *World Book Encyclopedia*, missed was that our biological clocks aren't on sun time. The circadian day for humans is longer than the solar day, which means that circadian time segments shift throughout each solar day. There is no one-to-one correspondence. The internal rhythms occur at different solar times each day. Have you ever been ravenously hungry in the middle of the afternoon for no apparent reason? Have you ever just not eaten lunch at your workday's "noon" because you weren't hungry? These are indicators of the circadian rhythms' impact upon our activities.

By tuning in to my own clocks as well as those of my employees and making observations everywhere I went, I could see that our internal rhythms are not preempted at all by either civilization or the sun's day. The body's day patterns, shifting through the 24-hour time segment our sun has so kindly provided, oscillate along a different, but trackable, time line. The river of the rhythm flows through our days, influencing our decisions to buy and sell, to eat and sleep, exercise and rest in definable, repeating segments.

Thoughts to Actions

Calling upon the expertise of professionals in clinical psychology, advertising, marketing and many other fields, we worked to discover a system that would work for everyone. Interestingly enough, I found that most scientists and much of the general public know about and accept the fact of these particular rhythms, but no one had mapped out the impact they have on individuals. No one had done the statistical analysis necessary to discover all the areas biological clocks define. Certainly no one had applied the knowledge to increase the productivity of a company or even of an individual.

The discovery we made—the effect of circadian rhythms on human behaviors and how to apply this information to daily productivity—has evolved into the *Optimum Performance Schedule*, or OPS, as I call it. With OPS, you can learn to use your biological clock to incredible advantage. With the information you find here, you will be able to increase your chances of meeting your productivity goals by as much as 90 percent.

In this book I will share with you more of my own story and those of many others whose lives have been profoundly and wonderfully affected by my system. I've been able to apply OPS to sales, crime statistics, medicine and even the stock market! We will explore the range of fields impacted by OPS and how individuals working in these fields can use the system to their advantage and that of their company. Literally every person in every field can benefit from the OPS system because of its universal impact.

OPS: Optimum Performance Schedule. It has changed my life. It can change yours.

ONE

OPSTIME

Charting Peak Performance Times

If you knew a way to insure that you would work at maximum productivity, up to potential, and produce optimum results, wouldn't you grab it?

Think how wonderful it would be if the people who work for you and with you could work smarter because they *know* when their peak performance times will occur on any given day. Think how terrific it would be if you could become a better producer yourself! OPS has applications for virtually every industry, every sales and marketing department, every entrepreneur and every business—from giant corporation to independent contractor, those with products and those with services.

Using this technology, you can now know when, on any given day and time during a coming month, to most successfully:

* make a sale
* hold a sale
* negotiate the best contract
* play the best game
* solve a complex problem

* present the best proposal
* perform surgery
* make investments
* place radio and television advertising
* increase or decrease staff
* avoid getting a traffic ticket

Or any other productivity goal! How, you ask? Let me show you.

The Search

As I attempted to "crack the code" governing the circadian time segments moving through each day, I delved into a number of studies on biological clocks. Since the area of chronobiology is such a relative newcomer—a mere 35 years old—many of these studies were considered experimental and not applicable to medicine as a whole. Even ten years ago, a provocative article appeared in the venerable *New England Journal of Medicine* appealing to the medical profession to make more use of the new understanding of the circadian day's organization of time. Today, scientific breakthroughs have generated increasing interest from the medical community in the workings of biological clocks. Physicians are beginning to connect the behavior of many diseases with the rhythm of the circadian day. Interest has arisen because every living organism runs on an internal clock that informs it when to eat, sleep, look for food and process it. Even cells divide on these biological clocks.

The link between OPS and biological clocks involves circadian clocks more directly than it does the other two categories of biological clocks—the *ultradian* and *infradian* clocks. But beneath all three categories, scientists have identified a huge network of hundreds of inner clocks, all responding to intricate timing mechanisms that keep each clock in balance with the others.

The circadian clocks tick in rhythm to the ultradian, which keep time most minutely. Ultradian clocks govern, for example, the milliseconds between the firing of neurons in brain cells, and the 90-minute cycles regulating our sleep and other processes.

All of our inner clocks march in time to the infradian tickers, which measure the larger cycles of seasons and life spans. Infradian time influences us in various ways, perhaps the most striking of which can be seen in the behavior of certain diseases:

* In March, 40 percent more cases of prostate cancer are diagnosed than at any other time of year.
* In April, infectious diseases in children—mumps, rubella, chicken pox and even measles—are at their height. Suicides also peak at this time.
* In May, 30 percent more cases of breast cancer are diagnosed than at any other time of year.
* Deaths from all causes peak during late February and early March.
* In spring, it's easier to lose weight than in fall. Eating disorders peak during both seasons.
* Heart and respiratory problems decline in the spring.
* Psychiatric and substance abuse problems peak in the spring from March through June.

These cycles, some of which also appear in the fall, have a remarkable connection not only to infradian clocks but also to the circadian rhythms. With OPS, I found that the six-month spring/summer cycle contains many more peak performance periods (times when you can best maintain your intensity, when your most important tasks should be scheduled) than the fall/winter cycle. I became convinced that the changes in the circadian rhythms during these seasonal shifts influence the infradian clocks. It's almost as if people hibernate during the winter—immune systems are down, people sleep more and, unlike the bears, they eat more. And calories turn to fat more easily in the winter cycle, too. When the cycles shift into full gear during March, a sudden accumulation of peak performance periods could have a cumulative effect—an observation borne out by the intensity of physiological and psychological events.

At this point, chronobiologists don't know what drives the clocks, or precisely what influence each has on the other. Do the big clocks drive the smaller ones? Or vice-versa? Is there some master timekeeper that sparks all the other clocks into motion?

The answer to this last question has been partly answered to some scientists' satisfaction, but not others. It seems that there is a cluster of some 8,000 cells attached to the pineal gland inside everybody's head that governs response to light. This mechanism is called, by those who can pronounce it, the suprachiasmatic nucleus, or SCN. One of two "master clocks" that appear to set all the other clocks, it is triggered by light, which in turn triggers a multitude of chemical reactions in our bodies. The interesting thing about this gadget is that the intensity of ordinary room light doesn't do it. Only sunlight works, even the most indirect—the crepuscular light just before dawn or the light on an overcast day. Scientists now believe that the SCN monitors and regulates the pendulums running most of our inner clocks.

But other scientists point to the fact that in experiments where people have completely shut themselves off from any natural light, their bodies still function much like they do in ordinary daylight. How can the SCN's dependence on light account for cues in the dark? Was there another "master" clock?

That's where OPS comes in.

Temporal isolation studies were done on both laboratory animals and humans at the Max Plank Institute in Bavaria. Volunteers lived in an apartment below the ground for as long as six months. The living space had no windows, no television and no telephone to call for the correct time. A newspaper was delivered when the isolated subject turned on the apartment lights, and there were plenty of books and writing instruments. It sounds like a writer's dream.

Bodily functions were monitored by the subject, who checked his temperature when he was awake during the "day" and drew blood samples according to his perception of the time. He ate when he was hungry and kept track of what and when he ate.

In the meantime, up in the real world, the subject's "day" was being compared to solar/lunar time. Results were exciting—time after time.

The subjects slid right into a circadian day. Without the trappings of society, work schedules, sunrise and sunset, the subjects reverted to keeping roughly 25-hour days. And as far as I have been able to ascertain, they awakened, slept, ate, read and exercised *within the OPS patterns created by the circadian rhythms.*

Many people have long been aware of inner clocks in their daily lives—jet lag, for example, is a result of out-of-phase internal clocks that were reset during the course of their stay, then reset again, in reverse, when they returned home. I thought if I could figure out how to use our inner clocks to stop that kind of fatigue, I would have something to shout about. Little did I know . . . .

Of all the studies I examined, though, *not one* was directed at understanding the impact of circadian rhythms on our practical, day-to-day life; none began to speculate on how to actually use the clocks to benefit a person's productivity. Why not? I decided to look for the answers myself, so I began to study the person I knew best—me. I set out to find my own optimum times.

I decided to map my own patterns of behavior according to the biological clocks. My wife thought I was diving off the board into an empty pool, but I persevered. I kept a record of what times of day I felt like sleeping, exercising and eating, and recorded what times management reports and sales were made and to what level of success. Because I traveled during peak times, I noted traffic accident reports on the radio. Also, I observed whether or not jet lag affected me.

My appointment book began to be stuffed with the times I did things. Then I began to visit people and places where I could get statistics on various areas. I became friends with police department and bureau of records employees, who gave me all kinds of lists and numbers. I obtained birth records dating back years. I talked to doctors and dentists, stock brokers and psychologists. I checked accident reports. I spent time at malls, especially on weekends and holidays, seeing when the crowds swelled and waned or when people seemed to be buying things. I figured all behavior was influenced by the biological clocks. If I could get enough raw data, I could see what was statistically significant, or at least important on a practical basis.

My employees were also part of my study. Making them unknowing victims to my statistical pursuits (since it had to be a blind study), I logged all their sales data, as well as my own. When my sales presentations to prospective clients went well, I made a note of the time. When they didn't, I recorded that in my day book, too—while I looked for a more auspicious time to do it over again.

The information I logged over a period of two years convinced me that I was on to something. I could see quite a database developing. My research showed that days are divided into four types of interrelated activity segments, each ranging between one and five hours. There are between seven and nine of these segments in any given circadian day. These segments vary in length and relationship to each other. As I had predicted, everything I had noted in my study corresponded to these time segments. Not only that, there were significantly more of certain activities during certain time segments.

With these preliminary results in hand, I decided to enlist the aid of professional consultants. It was a risk. Would the statistical data fall apart? Would clinical trials disprove my years of empirical observation, and fail to discern a significant and statistically viable pattern? Did statistically viable also mean practical? Would our human ability to reset our internal time frames with the rising and setting of the sun interfere with the results of my studies? And when all was said and done, could we find a pattern that repeated so that we could predict when these time segments would occur?

Combining the considerable talents of statisticians, clinical psychologists, medical, financial and marketing people in analyzing the influence of the circadian rhythms, we began constructing an extensive database. By charting behavior influenced by the internal clocks, a system emerged from the masses of numbers and times. It did not seem to have monthly or even yearly cyclical patterns, which is why no one had ever discovered precisely what the recurring pattern was.

During the course of our research, one of the most frustrating parts to put together was the patterning of the rhythms. What good were all these wonderful statistics if we could not predict future patterns?

The Final Key

During a meeting in my office, which was cluttered with papers, schedules and computer printouts mixed in with coffee cups and half-eaten snacks, I looked at the ceiling and said, "Maybe there is no pattern."

But once again we took our reams of data and submitted it to the cold analytical eye of the computer, thinking that it could discern what the human eye could not. After days of complex computer analysis, our theory was proven true. The computer had discovered the key. We had solved the riddle of the patterns that had influenced human behavior for so long. We could, at last, predict when the patterns would occur.

On a day-by-day, hour-by-hour basis, we could predict when were the best times for selling and buying, giving a presentation, increasing or decreasing staff—in fact, the possibilities seemed endless.

It would have been easy at that point to get carried away and rest on our initial conclusions. We were successful, and in the chapters ahead, we will share how the Optimum Performance Schedule that grew out of this research works, how it applies to you, your work, your health and your community.

We knew that ultimately this technology would become the way for an individual to zero in on any goal he might want to accomplish. Whether it's closing a sale, winning a friend, improving one's health, gaining an advantage in sports or business or just living the good life both professionally and personally—OPS could offer the answers.

The Formula for Success

The accuracy of the OPS formula rests solidly on the technology we have developed. It is based on a new kind of circadian calendar, one with a built-in schedule to optimize performance in every productivity area. We found the formula for the movement of human biological clocks and computerized it based on precision data.

With OPS, timing *is* everything. The impact of our biological clocks can't be overstated. Used to its fullest, OPS provides important information on planning events and scheduling appointments, making decisions and buying things. The data we have collected shows us that OPS can also predict what times of day more babies will be born, more accidents will occur and more crimes will be committed. OPS can even predict hourly trends on the stock market!

During our research we found that certain kinds of activities occur more often during one kind of time segment. Our technical team figured out the sequence of time segments and their relationships. The theory was validated by running them through statistical analyses to determine what events—such as homicides, accidents and births—took place in which kind of time segment. The results are an astounding coupling of behavioral and time studies.

Communicating this in an easy and sensible way stumped me until I realized the answer was right under my nose all the time—my day-planner book! I had been keeping track of much of my experience for several years, color coding each time segment. Out of this, a color system evolved which I can easily communicate to you. It makes OPS segments definable at a glance so that you will know when to schedule various activities to produce optimum results.

By this time you probably have some questions. You may even be a little skeptical. Let me share with you some of the most commonly asked questions.

Questions and Answers

Why hasn't anybody ever thought of this before?

People have thought about it. Doctors and biologists have discussed the implications in a few studies, and research continues at such places as the Max Plank Institute in Andechs, Bavaria. Subjects participate in experiments that remove them from the outside world. For 30-day periods, they live in small apartments without seeing the sun, a television or any other external time indicators. The studies are carefully monitored and controlled, and much information has been learned. But until we did it, no one outside of an academic or scientific setting had put together a statistical package detailing the effects of biological rhythms on our practical, daily lives.

Do time zones affect OPS?

Any time zone in the northern hemisphere works on exactly the same General Schedule you find in this book. When visiting other time zones, however, you will be on their time, which means resetting your biological clock to theirs. We have methods for dealing with that beginning on page 132.

Is OPS as simple as the circadian rhythms that I can look up in a biology book or the encyclopedia?

No. It would be wonderful if you could just look up circadian rhythms in the encyclopedia and decide to follow them to achieve productivity. Then we would not have had to spend all those years and dollars mapping, computing and analyzing and you wouldn't need OPS. Fortunately, we've already done the work for you. To quote one eminent authority, ". . . investigators believe that better knowledge of biological clocks and the rhythms they control will help scientists find ways to use the rhythms for our benefit." We have done that. And now you can benefit.

Is OPS the same as biorhythms?

No. A lot of people have heard of biorhythms, so that's the first question they ask. Biorhythms have no scientific basis; OPS is based entirely upon statistically probable, provable and practical data. Biorhythms fall into a gray pseudoscientific area. Its proponents claim that each individual has three cycles, beginning at birth and continuing unwaveringly until death. One's emotional cycle takes 28 days to complete, while the intellectual cycle takes a 33-day turnaround, and the physical ability waxes and wanes every 23 days. These cycles rise and fall, crossing each other at certain points, on which days a person is more likely to experience bad luck or accidents. Charting services sell many kits with which people can chart their own biorhythms, and consultants do personal charts.

Biorhythms are simply a theory, and one that has yet to be proven, even though it's been tried. The theory originated around the turn of the century in Germany, but remained largely dormant until the 1960s, when George F. Thommen wrote two books about biorhythms. The books were so popular and convincing that during the 1970s a dozen independent studies of such things as suicides and accidents were conducted by airlines and the military. No correlation with biorhythms was found.

The problem is simply that they were studying the wrong rhythms. When we applied our microscope to accidents and suicides, we clearly found the correlations they were looking for: See chapter 2 for the results of our investigations.

Is OPS based on astrology?

From time to time we are also asked whether OPS is based on astrology or magic. Astrology, though an ancient discipline, has no grounding for OPS. And, although everyone loves magic, OPS involves no sleight of hand. We are pragmatic people who believe what can be proven with established scientific methods and empirical evidence.

As a matter of perspective, however, we might suggest that ancient peoples would consider televisions magic, just as they believed mental illnesses were caused by demons. Today we recognize televisions as electronic products and diseases as biochemical imbalances which can be treated with the correct medicines. "Magic" in many cases is only undiscovered science, and there are many more things in the universe left for us to discover. OPS is based on existing scientific principles applied to our daily lives instead of abstract theory.

The Breakthrough

After the patterns had emerged, we felt we had to take our work one step further. Something as earth-shaking as this needed to be protected because of its enormous benefit and value to society. What we had discovered was so revolutionary that we applied for a patent.

The results of all this as well as the other studies we did convinced me that the circadian rhythms had the status of a second "master clock." What this means to people is incalculable: *the Optimum Performance Schedule is keyed to one of the most important timing mechanisms in all of humanity.*

TWO

THE OPTIMUM PERFORMANCE SCHEDULE

How to Know When

In the midst of perfecting OPS, my friends and many of my clients and colleagues became as excited as I was over the program. Some wrote me on their own, and others were asked to document how they used OPS in their own lives. I received a letter from my colleague Harry Hedberg, who for many years was senior vice president of marketing for Federated Department Stores' Rich's Division and now owns Rainbow Total Marketing Group, a successful agency in Atlanta established in 1980.

Dear Bob,

The value of "time" as a marker on my personal and professional lives has never been greater.

Time itself is simply a measurement. Timing is strategic use of that commodity—and the OPS technology has helped my company, Rainbow Total Marketing Group, take a giant step toward maximizing the productive use of time.

The opportunity to identify when to present a project has become almost as important as what's being shown. The world's oldest cliche—"timing is everything"—has become, "we can time anything," because of the breakthrough OPS has given us. We set meetings, presentations and all major projects by OPStime. I feel OPStime is a critical tool to any company where time and its strategic use are important.

From a personal standpoint, when you first presented the OPStime concept I was interested but not sold. That is, not until I put it to work on a personal basis. Now my OPSday timer goes with me everywhere and every time, including weekends. It provides an edge at any time increased productivity is in order.

This is the *advantage technology of the '90s. You have truly unlocked one of nature's secrets.*

Sincerely,

Harry Hedberg

Secrets Revealed

Watching people like Harry become believers as OPS reveals its secrets of timing is gratifying. As you discovered in the last chapter, OPS is based on the existence of circadian rhythms, but the true influence of these rhythms on our lives has remained a secret. What OPS does is expose the details of that underlying influence. We have discovered that the rhythms impact behaviors as subtle as impulsiveness, confidence and attention span. The behaviors we express in buying, selling and planning—just to name a few—are guided by the rhythms during definable portions of the day.

When people began finding out about my new technological time system, they insisted on trying it out for themselves. Their input helped me devise the simplest method of presenting it to you. So, let me introduce you to an OPS year. It's presented in a calendar format beginning on page 139 so that you can use it easily to begin scheduling your own daily calendars. It pinpoints, on an hourly basis, the four time segments in a circadian day. You can use it to mark your own day planners.

Understanding the Schedule

When most people look over the OPS schedule, their first reaction is usually a response to the color bars (see example on pages 25-26). They are curious about what happens to change the color, why there are only four colors and why we chose those colors.

The colors change because there is a shift in the circadian rhythms at those hours. The scientific studies that we examined charted sleep/wake/activity cycles during the circadian "day." Our research pinpointed the hours the shifts took place, and then assigned colors to them. I had actually already worked the color scheme out in my daybook during my own studies. My OPS team took my personal system and worked it out to match the rhythm streams of the new calendar. Since we found four kinds of shifts, the number of colors was automatically dictated by that. We named them *Optimum Gold* for peak performance times; *Excellent Green* for second-most intense performance times; *Moderate Blue* for the most objective times; and *Fair Red* for the least intense times.

Look at the sample of one day that we have lifted out of the main schedule.

7:00 a.m.	Optimum Gold
8:00 a.m.	Optimum Gold
9:00 a.m.	Fair Red
10:00 a.m.	Moderate Blue
11:00 a.m.	Moderate Blue
12:00 noon	Moderate Blue

1:00 p.m.	Fair Red
2:00 p.m.	Fair Red
3:00 p.m.	Fair Red
4:00 p.m.	Optimum Gold
5:00 p.m.	Optimum Gold
6:00 p.m.	Optimum Gold
7:00 p.m.	Optimum Gold
8:00 p.m.	Optimum Gold

It chronicles the hours from 7:00 a.m. to 8:00 p.m. because those are the hours when most work takes place. The missing hours have been charted in the General Schedule beginning on page 139, and they are of major importance to certain fields such as medicine and industries engaged in shift work, but we address these issues in specialized charts available by mail to interested parties.

The workday begins in Optimum Gold and changes to Fair Red at 9:00 a.m. A Moderate Blue time period takes over then at 10:00 a.m. and continues until 1:00 p.m. A major three-hour Fair Red segment until 4:00 p.m. is followed by an Optimum Gold until 9:00 p.m.

At first there appears to be little predictability about the time segments. The Optimum Gold time ending at 9:00 p.m. on that day runs from 6:00 p.m. to 11:00 p.m. the next day, and shows up again just hours later at 6:30 a.m., ending at 11:30 a.m. If all the segments would only move forward just an hour, breaking the circadian code would be easy. But they don't. The individuality of each day was one of the most puzzling elements we had to figure out when constructing the schedule. But after we located the key, it made predicting the future movement of the rhythms possible.

Color and Productivity

Having charted, mapped, analyzed and computed statistics and observations over several years, I have concluded that OPStime and productivity can be matched. Our research showed that certain behaviors dominate definable segments of the day. Certain color times are best suited for particular activities. For example, fund raising is best in Optimum Gold times, meditating achieves optimum results in Fair Red times.

Each color is keyed to a group of daily events. In my experience, it is easy to start thinking in terms of color and what activity is appropriate for each one.

There really is no good-better-best scale; each color segment simply represents a better time for certain activities rather than others. For example, as you will see in chapter 3, a study I did with my company showed superior sales were made in Optimum Gold and Excellent Green time segments, with fewer in Moderate Blue. But watch out for those Fair Red times! They were a sure stop sign where sales were concerned.

On the other hand, the Fair Red segments, which run between one and three hours at a time, turn out to be the best times for resting, filing, sorting paperwork, traveling and taking care of matters such as sending back the Publishers' Clearing House sweepstakes entry form.

The beauty of the color scheme is that it can be used to denote relative intensity. Optimum Gold is relatively more intense than Excellent Green, which is in turn relatively more intense than Moderate Blue. Fair Red is by far the least intense time segment of OPStime. All you need to do is sort your activities in order of their importance and relative need of intensity, and schedule them accordingly.

Whenever possible, your most important activities should be scheduled during the most favorable time segment. In terms of energy intensity and opportunity for success, the color segments fall in the following order: Optimum Gold, Excellent Green, Moderate Blue and Fair Red. On subsequent pages you will find possible applications for each OPStime. The given times and applications are just examples. Since every human is unique, some time segments will be more productive than others for certain people. To quote automobile manufacturers, "Your mileage may vary." It is up to you to determine what activities require the best of your abilities and schedule your day accordingly.

On our sample OPS day, I would first consult the main schedule to determine when the color shifts occur. Were I planning that day, I might set up a 7:00 a.m. breakfast meeting during the Optimum Gold period. Despite the early hour, I can include high priority issues since I know people will be alert and ready to buy. What a great way to start a day! But the meeting would need to end by 9:00 a.m., when a Fair Red period sets in, lasting until 10:00 a.m. During this hour, administrative duties and organizational tasks could take precedence. A Moderate Blue period stretches from 10:00 a.m. until 1:00 p.m., indicating the most constructive time for creative thinking. The Fair Red segment, which dominates the afternoon from 1:00 p.m. to 4:00 p.m., may influence this afternoon negatively. Although most people are at their individual bodyclock's most productive time, they may feel out-of-sorts or even sleepy, unless they find an appropriate "Red" activity. But things should perk up around 4:00 p.m., when a five-hour Optimum Gold time appears. Meeting people, scheduling appointments, presenting reports, taking tests, performing lab experiments or surgeries—activities involving interaction with other people or the use of instruments—will be productive. This is the best time to close deals and make major presentations.

Unfortunately, a Fair Red period is not indicated between 5:00 p.m. and 6:00 p.m., the time usually considered rush hour. Our research shows rush hours in Fair Red times contain fewer accidents. The Optimum Gold times are the worst: No matter what the weather, rush hour during these times will mean additional staffing at 911 and very busy ambulance drivers. This day's rush hour in Optimum Gold tells me I have made a good decision to stay inside and negotiate deals.

At 6:00 p.m., I am meeting with potential new clients. I know they are ready to listen to my information and are receptive to buying my products. Rather than push for a close during this meeting, I will schedule a meeting in another Optimum Gold time to sign contracts if they decide to buy. A businessman with whom I have been negotiating a major contract is meeting me at 7:00 p.m. in my office. I know I can wrap up this discussion and take home signed contracts around 8:00 p.m. After this last appointment, my wife and I can have a good dinner, which will be terrific because food always tastes better at the height of an Optimum Gold time.

When the rhythms change to a Fair Red around 9:00 p.m., we'll be ready for a good night's sleep. Our ultradian clocks have begun feeding the hormone melatonin into our bloodstreams to slow us down and make us sleepy. The Fair Red time segment will increase the effects of this hormonal cycle.

Here's a sample of what my completed day's schedule looks like. It has been carefully planned to accommodate the behaviors that dominate each time period.

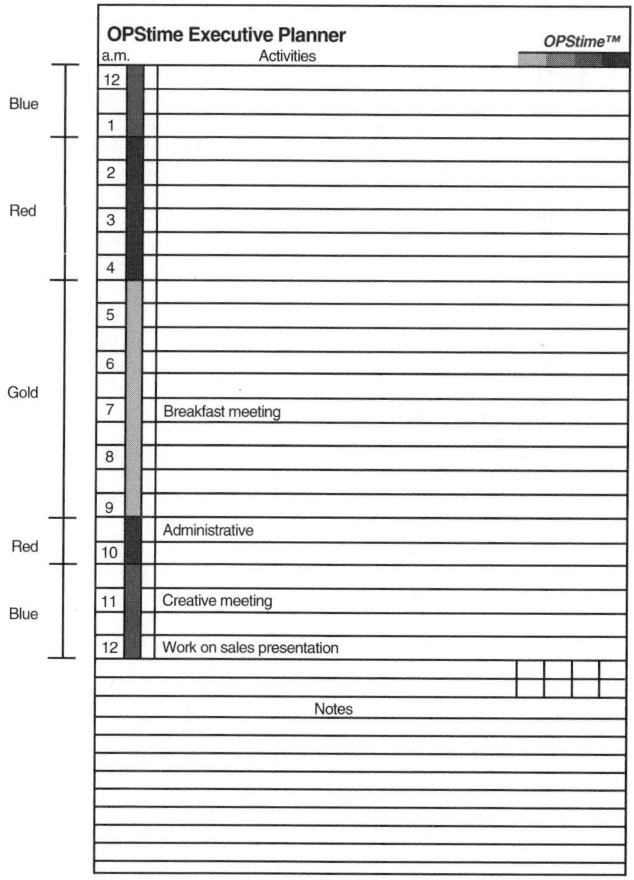
OPStime Executive Planner
OPStime™
a.m.
Activities
Blue
Red
Gold
Red
Blue
12
1
2
3
4
5
6
7
Breakfast meeting
8
9
Administrative
10
11
Creative meeting
12
Work on sales presentation
Notes

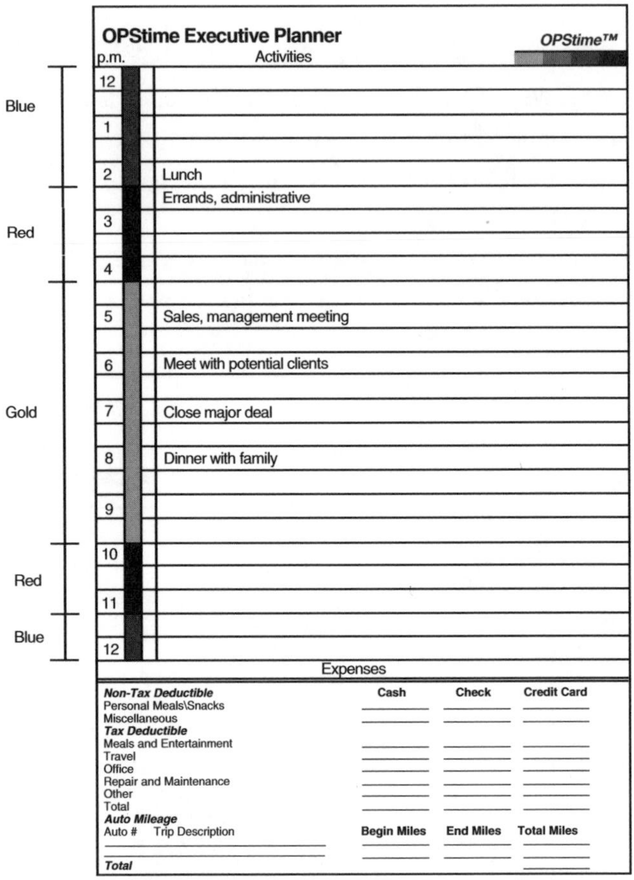
OPStime Executive Planner
OPStime™
p.m.
Activities
Blue
Red
Gold
Red
Blue
12
1
2
Lunch
Errands, administrative
3
4
5
Sales, management meeting
6
Meet with potential clients
7
Close major deal
8
Dinner with family
9
10
11
12
Expenses
Non-Tax Deductible
Cash
Check
Credit Card
Personal Meals\Snacks
Miscellaneous
Tax Deductible
Meals and Entertainment
Travel
Office
Repair and Maintenance
Other
Total
Auto Mileage
Auto # Trip Description
Begin Miles
End Miles
Total Miles
Total

What's Hot, What's Not

To give you a preview of the topics we will be detailing in the coming chapters, here is a list of things to do—and not do—in the four time segments. As you become more involved with OPS, you may add your own list of behaviors. These are some of the things that have worked for us.

For activities requiring the most intensity:

OPTIMUM GOLD

HOT	NOT
Selling anything	Impulse buying cold
Calls	Impulsive decisions
Performing surgery	Driving a car
Going to the dentist/doctor	Filing, paperwork
Any important meeting	Meditating
Playing any sport	Treating psychiatric disorders
Advertising placement	
Opening a restaurant	
Fund-raising	
Lobbying	
Teaching new material	
Retail sales	
Strategy meetings	
Feeding nursing home residents	
Accidents	
Homicides	

For important activities requiring less intensity than Optimum Gold:

EXCELLENT GREEN

HOT	NOT
Sales and sales meetings	Meeting new clients
Meeting established clients	Field training
Systems analysis	Abstract thinking

Training salespeople	Designing new programs
Management meetings	
Building, working with hands	
Industrial shift work	
Counseling	
Hiring	
Purchasing decisions	
Accounting	
Financial forecasting	

For activities requiring moderate intensity:

MODERATE BLUE

HOT	NOT
Writing	Routine paper work
Creative meetings	Accounting
Working with ideas	
Planning meetings	
Conferences	
Major decisions	
Designing	
Sales, marketing	
Treating psychiatric disorders	

For activities requiring the least intensity:

FAIR RED

HOT	NOT
Meditating	Major decisions
Sleeping, resting	Selling anything
Filing	Important paperwork
Non-critical paperwork	Strategy meetings
Driving a car	Learning or teaching new material
Long-distance travel	Purchasing decisions
Window shopping	Designing new programs
Solving practical problems	Buying media
Organizing	Feeding nursing home residents
Running errands	
Rearranging computer files	

From this short list, you can begin to add examples on your own. Behaviors fall into groups: the Optimum Gold times will always contain assertive modes while Excellent Green times are more mellow. Excellent Green times are better for weighing decisions you might have made during the intensity of the Optimum Gold time. The Moderate Blue segments are good for more objective activities, but are still very productive. They can be used for sales or to put down your innovative ideas about how to manage your office better or to come up with that new product hanging around the back of your mind. Fair Red times were given to us for R&R—you can use this time to go to lunch. You probably won't eat as much. One of our continuing OPS studies involves the best time to diet . . . but that's one of our subjects in the next book!

As you can see from the previous examples, there are numerous applications for the various OPS times. It may take a little trial and error to ascertain what is best for you. I have attempted only to give an example of what works for me. You must determine what is best for your individual and business situations. I have by no means tried to encompass all the possible applications for OPS time segments. The uses for OPS and the ways to prioritize your activities are limited only by your imagination. A simple rule of thumb is to "Go for the Gold." When possible, try to plan your most important activities or meetings in Optimum Gold. Your next best choice would usually be Excellent Green, followed by Moderate Blue. It is as simple as that.

THREE

ON TIME SALES

One of the greatest salesmen I ever knew—a Harvard graduate, talk-show host and owner of a well-established company—was one of my unwitting victims in the blind studies conducted by my company. Later, when he came to understand the power of OPS, he wrote to me:

Dear Bob,

Two years ago you told me you had discovered a scientific method by which you could predict the time frames in which individuals or groups could anticipate peak performances in their work.

Skeptical, I agreed to help you form a model for your method with myself as willing victim. I told myself that if there was even a remote chance I could improve my sales to 90 percent of my potential, what could I lose?

As you well know, it did not take long to turn my doubtful stance into a believing one! Your empirical study in "real world" applications was amazing. I improved my sales 50 percent in just a few months—and that was early in the program. Since that time, I have had to extend my "potential" several times; I had no idea my abilities could take me this far.

Your results were predictable and consistent, and I can duplicate performances. This is a powerful program; I can only begin to imagine the list of applications. Think how important this system would be to the surgeon planning an operation, to an athlete in competition, or especially to a President negotiating a treaty. For my life, it has had the impact of the discovery of electricity.

Thank you for letting me in on the ground floor of this system. It has meant the world to me, and I'll be glad to be a willing victim for any of your future projects.

Sincerely,

Bob Hall

Bob was willing to open his mind to a different way of thinking about time—especially when things began to work in his favor. I appreciate his cooperation. After all, the whole thing began as just a curiosity.

From the Second Floor, Straight Up

For the past twenty-four years, I have been a residential and commercial building contractor. My family before me had been entrepreneurial for several generations, and in the building trades for many years. So, in a sense, I was able to start on the second floor. But it was OPS that allowed me to reach the top.

One of my companies' products include building and siding materials for exteriors. The corporate structure runs the gamut from marketing experts and management to day labor. Our portfolio was one of the largest in Georgia before I discovered OPS, but implementing the OPS system improved closed sales by 25 percent annually. Like my friend Bob Hall, we had to redefine our goals many times because we kept surpassing our own forecasts.

The arrival of OPS in my life came at exactly the right time; this company was in a good position to grow and change. But I needed just the right thing to boost sales. Having experienced the ups and downs of our national economy during all kinds of financial and political conditions has given me a certain perspective on business. Nothing succeeds like experience. It has made me a keen observer of trends and involved me in a great deal of forecasting. I thought my forecasting abilities were pretty good, given the success of my companies. But that was before I knew that OPS could be a much more accurate forecaster.

Because we can now schedule our sales appointments during times we *know* will be most effective, my companies can combat the elements of economic and legislative variations. OPS has provided us with stability in an exciting and ever-changing business climate.

Change, Adapt and Care

Three other ingredients enhance the magic of OPS in my formula for success: Change, adapt and care. Now that I have the OPS system, *changes* are far more predictable than they used to be; now I can anticipate and plan my *adaptations* to changing business trends. The one constant in this mix is the *care* I take of my employees. I have always measured my success with them by a low turnover rate. OPS has enhanced the workday at my company by increasing sales, promoting a better understanding of work habits and helping my employees with their time management.

Using OPS has made my company a true leader. In the building trade, the national sales average runs about 33 percent. But actual sales drop to about 16 percent because of the "kick rate," which is a loss of sales due to decision changing or bad credit or a number of other factors. OPS has produced *actual* sales in my company of 35 percent of leads—including the kick rate.

I constantly entertain new ideas, seek them out and weigh the consequences of their use. As OPS developed, I could see that it was going to be a system that matched my ideal criteria: if it's good for me, it's got to be good for you. If that sounds old-fashioned, that's okay. It works.

The Old and the New

When I look back to the days before OPS, I see a company doing well, but in need of order. OPS has provided that and more. To help establish the system, we spent a portion of two years on two intensive sales and productivity studies to validate my original empirical observations about circadian rhythms. The first study involved a deliberate effort to schedule appointments in optimum times. The second was an historical study, involving a close analysis of our appointments and sales records from the period before I began studying biological rhythms and time segments.

For the first study, I set up a system whereby I could watch data and collect it by using my sales force, which did not know that it was being studied.

At this company, the people who make the appointments for the salespeople fill out lead slips, which have dates and times of appointments. Our logs tell whether the appointment was sold. That was all the information I needed to test the interplay between times of day and circadian rhythms.

To test the effectiveness of particular times, I had the operators set appointments during the times I had marked on the calendar. The times coincided with my Optimum Gold, Excellent Green, Moderate Blue, and Fair Red periods.

Then I watched what happened.

The first trends appeared to be better sales, and the comments from salespeople pleased me. When appointments were scheduled in Fair Red periods, they blamed a "no sale" on everything from the weather to sinus conditions. Following Optimum Gold time appointments, they came back in the office with comments such as, "That was a great lead!" Sometimes they would come in and grouse about an appointment for nine o'clock on a Saturday morning—and then wonder why it had been such an easy sale.

I would usually wait until the end of the month when the percentage data was accumulated to do my statistical work. Armed with the logs, lead slips and a yellow legal pad, I recorded percents of leads to sales, percents of leads sold per salesperson, percentage of appointments to sales and the source of the lead. Then I would get out my daytimer and record the pertinent information in the time segments.

I only included the sales closed in one appointment. Many people call back weeks or even months later, but these sales were not computed into the study. It was too difficult to establish motivation, and the time of the decision could not be calculated.

Validating Results

After six months of this, I decided to do the historical study, too. While recording the ongoing data was proving spectacularly successful, I believed the journey back through time should conclusively prove my theory.

What I found knocked me over. There, accumulated in thousands of lead slips and logs, was all the validating information I could want. In some Fair Red times the sales were only four percent. In some Optimum Gold times, they were as much as 90 percent. The Fair Red times had only 14 percent overall closing ratios. But Optimum Gold and Excellent Green times had 72 percent and 54 percent closing ratios respectively! In all our innocence, we had made appointments, made and lost sales—all to the underlying but overwhelming forces of the circadian rhythms. To understand the true drama of the effect of OPS, look at the chart on the next page. Sales are so far down in the Fair Red times that I decided those are definitely not the times to sell my products.

Even more exciting, when I mapped the results of my ongoing control study, the statistics were *exactly the same!* (See graph on page 37.)

The OPS program indicates the times when people are most receptive. We're always talking about increasing our own productivity, but the fact is that the eyes and ears of the potential client are always more receptive during OPS Optimum Gold, Excellent Green and Moderate Blue times. People are more likely to buy at these times, whether we are terrific salesmen or not. I had a man who sold for me briefly. He was really in the wrong field, and not a gifted salesman. But even he could sell my products during the best OPS times!

Robert S., on the other hand, is a very talented salesperson. A look at Robert's sales percentages (see chart on page 38) during the individual studies I made on each salesperson revealed some fascinating information. Robert was a very creative person, as his approach to sales reflects. A frustrated architect, Robert could make small changes in the client's home that made major differences in the efficiency and look of the house. Robert's largest percentage of sales relative to a time period were in Moderate Blue periods, with Optimum Gold periods running a close second. I expected high sales in the latter, but the Moderate Blue period's sales were interesting to me. I wondered if there was some correspondence between his creative nature and his ability to perform well during that time. (The results of my curiosity became part of chapter 7.) But Robert's sales during Fair Red periods? They mirrored the rest of the company.

Look at a typical day in Robert's working life. In the OPS time segments for that day, we find that a five-hour Optimum Gold segment begins at 8:00 a.m. A heavy sales appointment schedule was set up for Robert by the sales operators for that period. The last appointment was slated to begin at 11:30 a.m. so that Robert could wind up the deal before the Fair Red time period began at 1:00 p.m. As luck would have it, the 11:30 a.m. client canceled, so Robert made a cold call and sold it! During the Fair Red time segment, which lasted until 2:30 p.m., Robert delivered contracts, grabbed a bite to eat and drove to his next appoint-

Taylor Construction Company
Percent of Appointments Sold
Results of Two-Year Study

Comparison of Percent of Day in Each OPS Time Relative to Percent of Appointments Sold During Each Time Segment

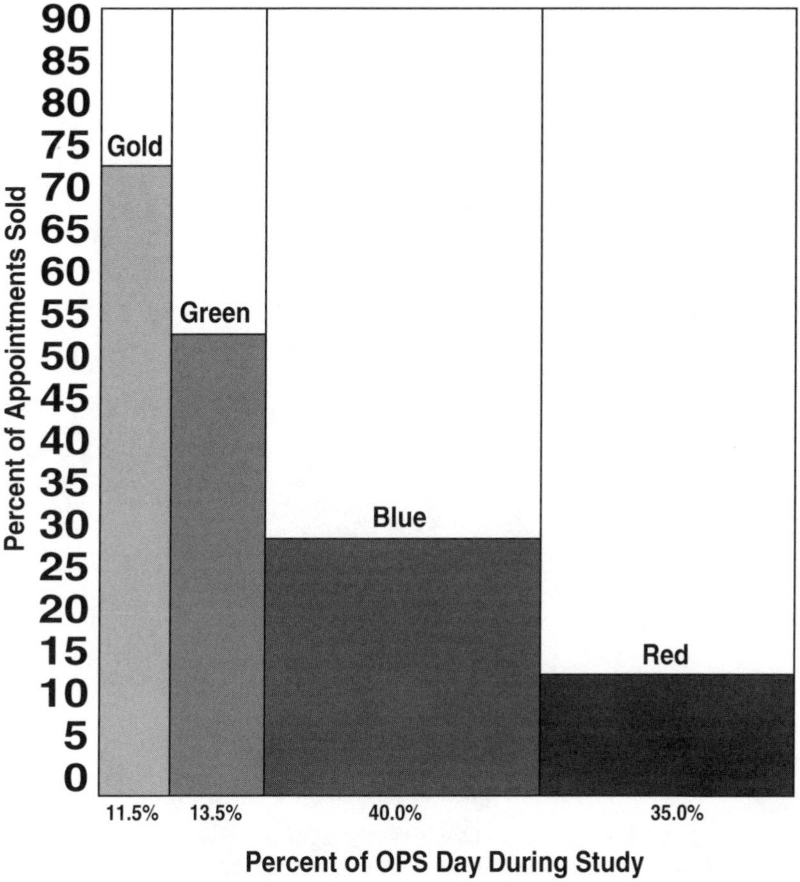

90
85
80
75
70
65
60
55
50
45
40
35
30
25
20
15
10
5
0
Percent of Appointments Sold
Gold
Green
Blue
Red
11.5%
13.5%
40.0%
35.0%
Percent of OPS Day During Study

Although gold periods were the shortest time segments in an average day during our study, the percent of sales closed relative to that time was 72 percent. Red times make up 35 percent of the day, but reflect only 14 percent of sales. We go for the gold!

Taylor Construction Company
Percent of Appointments Sold for Robert S.
Results of One-Year Study

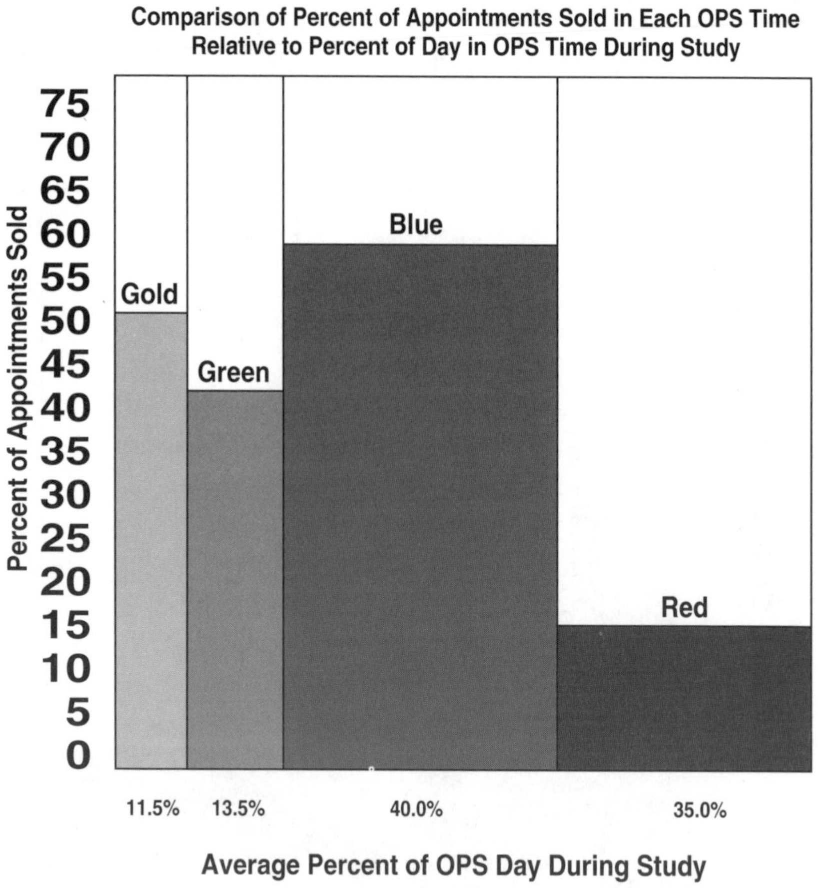
Comparison of Percent of Appointments Sold in Each OPS Time
Relative to Percent of Day in OPS Time During Study
Percent of Appointments Sold
75
70
65
60
55
50
45
40
35
30
25
20
15
10
5
0
Gold
Green
Blue
Red
11.5%
13.5%
40.0%
35.0%
Average Percent of OPS Day During Study

Robert's successful sales reached a high point during the blue times, in contrast to the statistics for the rest of the company. He closed sales in excess of 55 percent of the time relative to blue periods, with percentages of sales in gold times a close second, edging over 50 percent. Note, however, the similarity of his sales during red times with the rest of the company.

ment. His individual best selling time, a Moderate Blue segment, lasted from 2:30 p.m. until 5:30 p.m. on this day. He entered a Fair Red period at 5:30 p.m., during which he came back to the office to finish the day's paperwork.

While this may appear to be most people's average workday, Robert's was carefully planned to optimize sales results. No appointments or closings were set in or near the Fair Red times; paperwork was slotted there. This deliberate schedule does not just "happen" to be successful. Again and again, such appointment planning and time management has proven its reliability and effectiveness. And this success can be duplicated simply by checking the OPS Schedule ahead of time.

OPS Strategies for Better Sales

At first, OPS was targeted primarily at sales, since this company is driven by them. But because sales are completely integrated with the rest of the company, it became obvious that corporate structure, personnel, management and advertising could be positively affected by my new system as well. Because OPS impacts scheduling in every department, I could say—and not understate the case—that OPS runs the company.

At my companies, the OPS criteria for scheduling meetings is this: the most important meetings of any sort receive the Optimum Gold periods; strategy meetings get Excellent Green or Moderate Blue, sales get all three. I hope I never have to schedule a focus group in a Fair Red time again. In my experience, the outcomes are nearly always disastrous. But there are many Optimum Gold, Excellent Green, and Moderate Blue times in most workdays, so that our sales schedules can maximize the opportunities for optimum performance. After all, without sales, there wouldn't be any meetings!

In my office I have a small chart which I use to plan every meeting. It's very simple:

This organizational structure prioritizes issues and implements the

Meeting Type	OPS Time
Critically important	Optimum Gold
Sales	Excellent Green
Focus groups	Excellent Green
Management	Excellent Green or Moderate Blue
Creative think tanks	Moderate Blue
Organizational/structural	Fair Red

OPS system effectively. A more detailed analysis of the reasons for assigning each meeting type a particular time segment is provided in subsequent chapters.

For me, adapting to change means improving my method. I have always been excited by the potential of any change, and non-traditional methods have a certain appeal for my maverick sensibilities.

For example, when telemarketing became the tool most people in my business used, I decided to use non-traditional methods because of the local overload on telemarketing. Plus, everybody I knew despised those 7:00 p.m. phone calls from somebody selling something! I went into radio and television, using celebrity endorsements, and enjoyed better results than any of the competition. When I added OPS to that, we decided to buy air time only during Optimum Gold, Excellent Green and Moderate Blue times. The outcome was even more dramatic improvement. In this case, OPS made a non-traditional approach one that is sure to have a long tradition at my companies.

I have four other primary non-traditional strategies for sales. OPS improved the performance over time in each case.

1. The one-time close isn't always necessary. In many businesses, if you can't sell the product, whether it's a car or a dress, the sale is counted as lost when the client leaves. When we visit with a potential client, we sell on strength of service, product knowledge and reputation. I do not insist that the account executive come back with a contract after the first appointment. OPS enables appointment flexibility here, because some people seem to insist on scheduling in a Fair Red time (see the next page for advice on overcoming this drawback). The interesting thing about this strategy is that now that we primarily schedule in Optimum Gold, Excellent Green and Moderate Blue times, we often close the deal in one appointment anyway!

2. Keep going back until they buy. Most people we see know deep down that they need our products. It's just a question of when. With OPS, we know for certain when the most opportune time is. Now it takes fewer callbacks, increasing both efficiency and number of sales.

3. Talk to clients in person. We never give our potential clients a price over the telephone. This allows us to form a one-on-one relationship with our client. Scheduling in the right OPS time enhances the chemistry of the encounter.

4. Grow, change and improve. OPS is the best improvement imaginable, but I won't stop there. For example, new products: We look at every one. Products are the cutting edge. They help sales because they are different and we can use them in advertising. OPS has shown us the right time to look at new products—Fair Red times. Using the OPS system to its full advantage, we know we will be able to carefully analyze new products in this time segment because we won't be in buying mode. Instead, we will take our time and look objectively at the product we are considering.

There's a Wrong Time for Everything

In my business, we try to set our appointments in Optimum Gold, Excellent Green or Moderate Blue times, but occasionally people just won't cooperate and insist on setting it in a Fair Red time. This is because they don't know about OPS. If a salesperson says something like, "We'd like to meet with you at another time because we know you will be more likely to buy then," the chances are good an appointment won't occur at all! So, we have developed several techniques to overcome the problems of bad timing.

* Don't close. As you know, the cycle of presentation includes the identification of the problem, your solution, overcoming objections and the close. Although it may go against your grain, present your solutions to the client's objections and then let him think about it.

* Call back during an Optimum Gold, Excellent Green or Moderate Blue time. If you haven't heard from your customer, contact him during one of the best times—if you need a third appointment, do your best to set it up in another optimum time.

* Listen. This goes for any salesman in any situation, of course, but in a Fair Red period, it becomes critical. Understand that your client won't be in a mood to hear you, so you must take great pains to hear him. Take notes. You'll need them at your next appointment.

* Ask noncommittal questions. Since this is not the time to press toward a sale, just gather background. People will sense your relaxed and helpful attitude.

* Don't give the product away just to make a sale. That's forcing it, and you will do much better if you let the strength of your product, service and reputation make its impression.

* Make the least important appointments during these hours. Let the Fair Red appointments be exploratory, not critical.

* Blame the right thing. It isn't the weather, sun spots, or a poor lead, and it certainly isn't you that failed to make that sale. It just may be the wrong time of the circadian day.

* Keep on going. The world isn't going to stop because sales go down during Fair Red times. The longest they can last is three hours.

Questions and Answers

How can I make OPS work immediately?

Look at next week on your day calendar. Consult the OPS General Schedule beginning on page 139. If you like, mark your daily calendar with colored markers to indicate the time segments. To begin, schedule your most important meetings in the Optimum Gold times, then Excellent Green, then Moderate Blue. This is really a simple program that can be very productive for you. As your sophistication increases, your productivity will rise even further. Check out the box on page 40 to prioritize your days.

Does OPS work for all kinds of sales?

I haven't found a sales program it did not enhance. To me, the whole economy is built on sales. Every single product and service, from wire cables to psychotherapy, depends on some kind of sale. OPS works for all of these—and the people who sell them.

What happens when the time shifts to another color segment during a sales presentation?

If you've ever been sailing along on a presentation and suddenly the whole thing falls apart for no apparent reason, you may have experienced a color shift, probably from Optimum Gold to Fair Red. I have appointments set up to start one and a half hours before the Optimum Gold, Excellent Green or Moderate Blue time period ends. Our presentation lasts that long, and I know that when a Fair Red period follows, the likelihood of losing the sale goes up dramatically. If you can, close before the time shift. If you can't close in time, use the methods outlined on page 42. If you begin a presentation during a Fair Red period, however, and shift to another during your presentation, the results can be excellent.

When should I see old, established customers?

If you are going to present a brand-new product even with old customers, go for an Optimum Gold or Excellent Green time. If the customer is simply placing a standard order, settle for a Moderate Blue time. There is less stress and less sell involved, and your relationship is already set.

When should I make cold calls?

At the absolute peak of the Optimum Gold times.

If there is a Fair Red time in the middle of my day, what do I do with it?

Plan, drive to the next appointment, do paperwork, file, set appointments for better times, send out follow-up letters.

I'm a nine-to-five salesman. Are there enough optimum times for me to really use OPS effectively?

OPS is connected to a rhythm in which the optimum times constantly move. If you could look at circadian rhythms, they might look like an old-fashioned barber pole, constantly revolving red and white stripes moving into infinity in both directions. Fair Red times ordinarily occupy some 35 percent of the day, with Optimum Gold, Excellent Green and Moderate Blue times moving around them. So, even though some workdays have three-hour Fair Red times in them, for example, you can be assured that this segment will move out of your critical time sequences in a few days.

As a floor salesperson on commission, how can I maximize sales when I have no control over when people come in?

When you are locked into walk-in customers, it's tough. But remember that people coming in are driven by the same undercurrent of circadian rhythms as you are. They are going to buy in the Optimum Gold, Excellent Green or Moderate Blue times. The casual shopper in a Fair Red time will turn into a serious buyer in the Optimum Gold. And all the rest of the serious buyers will storm the front doors when they feel compelled to buy. Look for those times and look your best.

I sell real estate. How can I adapt OPS to my schedule?

At times you have multiple meetings, and you may not be able to avoid Fair Red times. Initial showings could be done in Optimum Gold and Excellent Green times; bank closings can be done in Fair Red times. It may be beneficial to your seller to negotiate contract conditions and punch lists in Fair Red times, too. Buyers won't be so hungry for the deal and will be less likely to drive bargains for expensive changes. Avoid Fair Red for talking to people who want to sell their houses.

FOUR

MANAGING ON TIME

Each American business is shaped like an equilateral triangle. At one angle, we find the thinker, the person who invented the idea for the business. This is the big picture person, the leader. In the second angle fits the financial officer. Over in the third angle we find the manager, who must produce the big picture in reality according to a budget determined by the financial plan.

As the "doers" of the operation, managers often find themselves walking the line between federal and state regulations, corporate headquarters, bosses, employees and customers. Matching the vision, the finances and company goals while managing all the details to create a win/win situation is an arduous task. The elements of business structures are hard to balance, and managers often find themselves responding to minute-by-minute pressures and losing precious time for planning and implementing well-thought-out strategies. The primary complaint I hear so often is, "It's as if my days are management crisis rather than crisis management."

How can OPS clear away some of the details that bury many managers in crisis management? How can OPS balance being reactive to crisis and proactive in making the company's mission work better?

OPS can produce the best results for managers by predicting when, on an hour-by-hour basis, people will be most receptive, objective or absent-minded. Spending a few minutes each week to plan the next week using OPS could bring measurable results quickly.

Any manager who must communicate with personnel or customers is a candidate for OPS. Because the circadian rhythms affect personality, managers can begin to connect the four OPS time segments to behaviors they see around them and respond accordingly.

By looking at the general events that managers must supervise each day and assigning the best OPS time for each, prioritizing becomes easier. An average day in the life of any manager includes meetings, supervision, project planning and implementation, computer time, phone calls, paperwork and presentations. By matching the task to the best OPS times, a manager can increase effectiveness manyfold.

OPS ACTIVITY CHART

Activity	Best OPS Time
Responding to crises	Chart, page 49
Important meetings	Optimum Gold
Project presentations	Optimum Gold
Important problems, not crises	Excellent Green
Projects with deadlines	Excellent Green or Moderate Blue
Planning	Excellent Green or Moderate Blue
Computer time	Excellent Green or Moderate Blue
Projects without deadlines	Moderate Blue
Less important meetings	Moderate Blue or Fair Red
Phone calls (non-crisis)	Fair Red
Mail	Fair Red
Inter-office visitation	Fair Red
Non-critical paperwork	Fair Red

Best Strategy Analysis

After determining the types of crises you must resolve, match each kind to the OPS analysis in the chart below. As you check your OPS day with the General Schedule (beginning on page 139), be aware of which time segment you are in as you move through your day.

OPS Time Period	Best Strategy
Optimum Gold	Because this is the most intense time in the circadian day, overreaction may be the key factor. Because you are aware of this, you can expect this situation and defuse it. Thinking clearly, making a plan and presenting it can be done most effectively at these times if anxiety has been removed.
Excellent Green	Crises taking place during this time segment may be handled more calmly because this time segment is less intense than gold. Objectivity, a valuable asset for any manager, holds sway during this period. Managers will find it easier to break the crisis into its components, and deal in the order of priority with those that can't be delegated.
Moderate Blue	In this even less intense circadian period, crises may seem mild compared to those occurring in the intense Gold times, and they can be handled with the same objectivity found in the Green periods.
Fair Red	Have you ever said calmly, "I'm not going to deal with this now," when confronted with a crisis and overloaded with everything else? Because this is the least intense time, it may even be difficult to ascertain if a crisis has indeed occurred. Feelings of lethargy and fragmentation are common during this time, and if action on the situation can be moved to a Green or Blue time period, which often follows Red quite shortly, results may be more favorable.

The rest of this chapter discusses the schedules of two very different kinds of managers in their day-to-day operations. We will look first at Bill Mink, a restaurant manager, and then at Diane Wilson, a human resources manager for a nationwide telecommunications company. These two people run the gamut from hands-on involvement in a direct service to a more distant, abstract and theoretical approach to management. By studying how Bill and Diane respond to working with the OPS calendar, you can learn to apply their approaches to your personal schedule. Their days typify the challenges of management.

Managing a Restaurant

Bill Mink manages a well-located, nationally franchised restaurant near a mall in a medium-sized eastern city. This chain is popular for families and others who want a good, reasonably priced dinner in a white-tablecloth atmosphere. It has been in business for many years, so its operations have become a well-oiled machine. The only unpredictable quotient is how many people will come to eat in the restaurant per week. Even taking weather considerations into account, Bill can only predict within about 200 people the number his restaurant will serve in any given week.

OPS can increase his forecasting accuracy. We worked with Bill on an historical study in which he supplied us with the numbers of customers per half-hour each day in random weeks. We matched these totals with our OPS calendars for those dates. Even given that workday lunches are usually taken between 11:30 a.m. and 1:00 p.m., and that dinners usually fall between 5:30 p.m. and 7:30 p.m., OPS trends appeared immediately.

Generally, dinner times seemed to have denser customer traffic than lunches, but our study overturned that misconception. Optimum Gold lunches beat Fair Red dinner hours although traffic was expected to be heavier at dinner. Overall, Optimum Gold times beat Fair Red periods by almost 50 percent. Excellent Green and Moderate Blue bested Fair Red by 18 percent. Conclusion? People go out for meals in Fair Red times at a sharply reduced rate from other periods. We can make the following conclusions for Bill:

* **Optimum Gold:** Optimum traffic
* **Excellent Green:** Excellent traffic
* **Moderate Blue:** Moderate traffic
* **Fair Red:** Fair traffic

Average Number of Customers Per Hour During Peak Meals

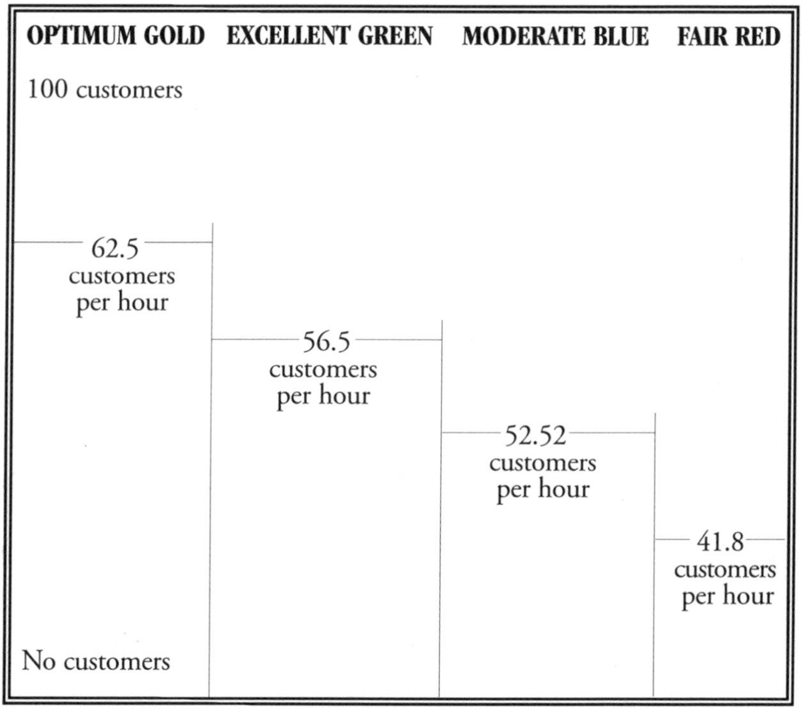
OPTIMUM GOLD
EXCELLENT GREEN
MODERATE BLUE
FAIR RED
100 customers
62.5 customers per hour
56.5 customers per hour
52.52 customers per hour
41.8 customers per hour
No customers

We suggested Bill pay attention to time segments preceding a Fair Red time to take advantage of the carryover effect. And when Fair Red shifts to Gold, Green or Blue, he can wait for the traffic to build.

Bill is excited about working with OPS because of the money it can save his restaurant in terms of staffing, wasted food and taxes. In being able to increase the accuracy of his projections, his operation's performance over time will look very good indeed to corporate headquarters.

Because of his business's structure, Bill's schedule cannot be rearranged to take advantage of the circadian rhythms, even though his is an area that responds most specifically to them. Instead, he must use OPS as a *reactive* tool, since people will be coming to his restaurant according to their biological clocks, particularly on weekends. The following schedules represent the luncheon and dinner shifts, which Bill works alternately. The restaurant is open from 11:00 a.m. to 10:00 p.m. daily, except on Fridays and Saturdays, when it closes at 11:00 p.m.

We chose these schedules because they are typical of thousands followed by restaurant and food service managers across the nation. We have selected a day from early summer to illustrate how to use OPS to approach management concerns when schedules are pre-set.

Bill Mink's Work Schedule

8:00 a.m. Fair Red	Arrive at 8:30 a.m. and check close from night before. Check food on hand.
9:00 a.m. Fair Red	Check production shift. Staff lets employees in. Review previous day's paper work, set up current day, and count safe.
10:00 a.m. Optimum Gold	Work on daily projections, check production, review pre-meal checklist and open store for lunch.

11:00 a.m. to 1:00 p.m. Optimum Gold	Opening manager monitors food production and kitchen activities. Mid-manager monitors dining rooms.
2:00 p.m. Optimum Gold	Make staffing cuts as volume decreases. Do afternoon paperwork, interviews, and have lunch with managers.
3:00 p.m. Fair Red	Finish production. Evening manager arrives, reviews log, counts safe, checks food for dinner, makes produce order, and sets next day's preparations.
4:00-4:30 p.m. Fair Red\Moderate Blue	Day manager prepares cash changeout, reviews evening staffing with manager, makes changes in evening shift. Evening manager monitors kitchen to assure readiness for dinner.
5:00-7:30 p.m. Moderate Blue	Day manager leaves. Evening managers monitor service in kitchen and dining rooms.
7:30-9:00 p.m. Fair Red	Begin kitchen clean-up and trash run. Pull frozen products for overnight thaw.
9:00 p.m. Fair Red	Mid-manager leaves. Evening manager monitors dining room, assists cashier with closing out.
10:00-10:30 p.m. Fair Red\Optimum Gold	Close restaurant. Cashier completes nightly paperwork. Make evening food count.
11:00 p.m. Optimum Gold	Check close. Leave.

Notice that there is an Optimum Gold segment from 10:00 a.m. to 3:00 p.m., covering the noon lunch hour. During the dinner hour, we find a Moderate Blue period followed at 7:30 p.m. by a Fair Red. From an OPS perspective, the lunch hour will seat far more customers than dinner will. In fact, even though it's a Wednesday, people will still be coming in for lunch after 2:00 p.m.

In our historical study of the numbers of people eating in the four OPS time periods, Optimum Gold outdrew every other time segment. When Bill works with his OPS calendar for this day, he can make sure his lunch time will have additional staff, and that he takes care of as much of the afternoon's paperwork as he can, because the long Optimum Gold may interfere with his normal routine. Although he would ordinarily make staffing cuts at 1:30 p.m., he needs to tell his people that today's lunch will be long and they should not plan to leave before 2:30 p.m. Even during the Fair Red time between 3:00 p.m. and 4:30 p.m., some customers may trickle in for a late lunch because the powerful effects of the Optimum Gold have carried through: People make the lunch decision in a Gold time, but don't get to the restaurant until the Fair Red. This carryover effect is visible whenever a lunch or dinner hour begins in Gold, Green or Blue and changes in the middle to Red.

Today's OPS times are a good example of the carryover effect. The Moderate Blue period gracing dinner from 4:30 p.m. to 7:30 p.m. will most likely produce customers until about 8:00 p.m., after which business will fall off dramatically. The evening manager, aware that this situation can occur, prepares to make staffing cuts early and instructs the kitchen to begin clean up and trash runs perhaps as early as 7:30 p.m. He could also let the mid-manager leave early.

Within the framework of today's schedule, Bill is also aware of how customers and employees will interact with each other. He has observed that lunches, always rushed for most people, become even more so during Optimum Gold. People are looking at their watches and demanding faster service either verbally or by body language. Tempers can flare more easily during these times, so Bill is careful to assign his new waitperson to an area with fewer tables to cover. During the early morning Fair Red time, he let the chefs know that today would be a volatile day in the kitchen, so they should be careful about mistakes and let him know right away if he should schedule backup help.

As Bill continued to use the OPS program, daily becoming more aware of its potential for him, his workday became less stressful overall, and his daily projections became amazingly accurate. His employees were happy at how sensitive he had become to their needs, and his bosses were delighted at the increases in the bottom line.

A Director of Human Resources

Diane Wilson is the director of human resources in the eastern base for a national telecommunications company. This office employs about 300 people, one-third of whom are sales staff. The rest are in customer services, collections, and the engineering group. Her department, a start-up operation begun in 1989, consists of six people—herself, a benefits administrator, a recruiter, a payroll person, a clerk, and a trainer. Between 50 and 60 percent of her department's work is done by others in the department, a percentage she is trying to increase so that she can be more accessible to employees and take on more global planning functions. Her company is growing at a very non-recessionary rate of nearly 30 percent per year, a fact that impacts heavily on her position because of the numbers of people being hired.

Her job description covers a wide range of skills. Her responsibilities include a thorough knowledge of each job in her department as well as direct involvement in the following areas:

* writing job descriptions
* determining relative value of jobs and translating that into salary
* job posting
* recruiting
* compensation program
* benefits packages (administration and implementation)
* employee relations (sounding board function)

* affirmative action program
* dotted line to payroll function
* quality coordinator for market
* installing TQM (total quality management) training program
* planning to strategize the company's business plan

To understand Diane's managerial day, we looked at the motivating principles behind it. Her long-range goal is the implementation of the TQM, the mission of which is the democratization of her company. She is committed to the idea that businesses are no longer autocracies and that differences in people and their cultures can be embraced and celebrated. Having established this principle, the employees can then concentrate on meeting the demands and needs of the customers quickly and efficiently.

Diane wanted to prioritize her day according to this goal, and she wanted to know how OPS could help her function more efficiently given the parameters of her job. Her day bounces between situations as varied as dealing with an upset employee, concerned because her son's broken arm wasn't fixed properly by the health care provider, and investigating a situation involving the EEOC and a potential lawsuit, for which she must write the position paper.

From answering mundane questions to doing the major planning and implementation of larger management concerns, it's often a non-stop pressure-cooker. Diane felt constricted by the reactive nature of her day and wanted to become more proactive. Because OPS is a time-prioritizing system rather than simply a time-management method, Diane's use of the OPS calendar helped her achieve her objectives.

NON-OPS Monday for Diane Wilson

8:00 a.m.	Arrive 8:15 a.m. Talk to several employees already waiting with concerns.

9:00 a.m.	Staff meeting (9:00 a.m. to 11:00 a.m.) with directors from all departments.
10:00 a.m.	
11:00 a.m.	Reactive meeting with one department director to talk about issues brought up in staff meeting.
11:45 a.m.	Spontaneous meeting with retail manager.
12:00 noon	Take group of employees to lunch to celebrate a fifth anniversary with the company and resolve departmental issues.
1:00-2:00 p.m.	Pick up E-Mail messages. Return phone calls to employees and home office.
3:00 p.m.	Proactive meeting with another department director to discuss department issues and where department is headed.
4:00 p.m.	Meeting with an employee about to be fired. Though a mediocre salesperson, she is very distressed at the prospect of losing her job. This meeting is the result of playing telephone tag for days, but because it has become a crisis, Diane has to take time slotted for job evaluations and spend it on the employee.
5:00 p.m.	Meet with manager of customer care and attorney, consult with corporate counsel at 5:30 p.m.
6:00 p.m.	Meet with another supervisor. Take call from home office and talk to a few employees. Do a few E-Mail messages and go through regular mail. Plan for next day.
7:00 p.m.	Leave office.

About twice a week, Diane is able to shift her child care responsibilities to her husband and arrives at the office by 7:00 a.m. She considers herself an early morning person, and enjoys the quiet time afforded by the hour and a half before the rest of the employees arrive.

This strategy is not the only way for Diane to work more productively throughout the day. It is necessary for her to become somewhat more protective of her workday's time—not limiting her accessibility, but letting people know what times she will be available for whatever task is being demanded of her.

To take advantage of her ability to get to work early, we selected an unusual OPS day to rearrange Diane's average Monday. Most days contain about one-third Fair Red time, with the rest in Excellent Green and Moderate Blue, or in combinations of Optimum Gold with Excellent Green or Moderate Blue. For Diane we have chosen a deep summer day that contains all four time segments.

An OPS Monday for Diane Wilson

7:00 a.m. Optimum Gold	Arrive at office. Plan strategies to implement business plan, and detail agenda for staff meeting.
8:00 a.m. Fair Red	Address employee concerns, if any, 8:30-9:00 a.m.
9:00 a.m. Moderate Blue	Staff meeting. Because this is the third most intense time period, the agenda Diane prepared in the early morning Optimum Gold time can now be discussed very objectively. For this meeting to be most productive, she must be aware that this is the best time to plant ideas, not sell them.
10:00 a.m. Moderate Blue	

11:00 a.m. Moderate Blue	Instead of the reactive meetings with other directors over issues brought up in the staff meeting, Diane should meet with the employee about to be fired. The directors need think time, and Diane will be able to handle her employee more effectively. The employee may be able to reason better as well.
12:00 noon Fair Red	This is a great time for lunch because most people don't eat as much in Fair Red times. But Diane shouldn't try to resolve departmental issues during this meal as she did during her non-OPS Monday. Instead, she should keep conversation light and fun.
1:00-3:00 p.m. Fair Red	Returning about 1:30 p.m., Diane schedules her regular mail, E-mail, non-crisis telephone calls and computer time here. Only a top priority, first-rate crisis should interrupt this administrative time. Medium-intensity items should be moved to another time segment.
3:00 p.m. Excellent Green	This is when Diane needs to meet with the two department directors. She has a much better chance of convincing them of her ideas now.
4:00 p.m. Excellent Green	The meeting with another director to talk about the structure of his department and where it is headed will be fine here.
5:00 p.m. Excellent Green	Meet with manager of customer care and their attorney. Consult with corporate counsel at 5:30 p.m. Plan possible position letter.
6:00 p.m.	Check next day's OPS calendar and plan accordingly. Leave at 6:15 p.m.

Diane's average workday may give credence to the idea that some people spend all their time in meetings. But she can schedule time to make reports and handle the other duties outlined in her job description on other days. With OPS as her prioritizing guide, she has the opportunity to create more control over the things she can change and to be more responsive to the things she can't. We did not radically rearrange her average day, but we did show her how to take advantage of her time segments. In addition, she was able to deal with more situations in a more organized way.

Questions and Answers

My company frequently runs "Midnight Madness" sales. As national sales manager, I find stores in one area do well, and those in another do not. How could OPS increase the bottom line for us?

Sometimes people beat the doors down. Other times, the store gives a party and nobody comes. What's the difference? Most likely neither weather nor season. It probably depends on what circadian time it is. If headquarters schedules on OPS time, they might improve chances for a terrific sale all over the country by as much as 72 percent. How? By scheduling each sale during an Optimum Gold time respective to each time zone. Instead of running the sale from 6:00 p.m. to midnight on a night that suits management, wait for a five-hour Optimum Gold or Excellent Green in each respective time zone. By targeting the Optimum Gold and Excellent Green time segments, your bottom line has a much better chance of being black instead of red.

We offer our preferred charge customers a "private sale" before the store opens to the public. As manager of this department store, how can I plan peak sales?

Most retailers use private sales to boost business during the weeks between major holiday sales. They frequently do very well because of the exclusive caché being offered, but with OPS, they could do even better.

Scheduling one of these sales in an Optimum Gold segment—for example, one beginning at 8:30 a.m. and ending at 1:30 p.m.—would not only attract preferred customers before the store opens to regular customers, it would be the best time for the general public over the lunch hour as well.

I manage a regional warehouse construction/leasing operation. My business is very competitive on the leasing end because of rapid growth in some areas. How can I use OPS to my best advantage?

When you are able to schedule leasing contract negotiations and sales presentations for Optimum Gold or Excellent Green or even Moderate Blue times, you will have an unfair advantage over your competition. Keep a record of deals closed in Fair Red against all other times just as I did (see chapter 3). When you schedule such meetings, make sure you close before the next red period begins or you may lose the sale. I also suggest you adjust for your customer's time zone before beginning negotiations. If you are in your zone's Optimum Gold while they are in Fair Red, wait for your respective color periods to coordinate; they should do that within a few hours.

As manager of a temporary personnel service, I have abandoned time-management books that tell me how to schedule down to the very minute. I am more interested in matching people to positions and don't care how long it takes to do that. Won't OPS hang me back up on the hook of time management?

Stephen R. Covey, chairman of the Covey Leadership Center and the Institute for Principle-Centered Leadership, talks about the evolution of the time-management field in his book, *The Seven Habits of Highly Effective People*. He observes that, "The essence of best thinking in the area of time management can be captured by a single phrase: Organize and execute around priorities." I would say that is precisely what you are doing, and I am sure commitment to that philosophy has been rewarding for you. OPS follows this philosophy as well. While each day does break down into circadian time segments between one and five hours long, OPS presents a system of prioritizing by behavior patterns and by the intensity of each time segment.

Arranging a day on OPS is a matter of matching your highest priority items with Optimum Gold and progressing from there to the least important tasks during Fair Red.

For your purposes, matching people with positions could best be done in Optimum Gold and Excellent Green time segments. Perhaps you could reserve your interviews for Moderate Blues and administrative paperwork for Fair Reds. Three out of four of the time periods occur each day, and it is easy to begin arranging priorities in this manner.

The mall in which I manage a jewelry store has a policy that two people must be in the store until closing, at 9:00 p.m. There are many times I can manage by myself because there are only a few customers. Can I do anything about this?

Usually, this policy has to do with security. If that is not a factor, or you can work out other security options, perhaps you could talk with the management company that operates the mall about OPS. All the stores might want to institute a policy of decreasing staff during Fair Red times in the evening. Do your own time study of historical or ongoing sales during these times. It won't take long before you have enough information to get the people involved to sit up and take notice.

FIVE

MARKETING, ADVERTISING AND PUBLIC RELATIONS

To paraphrase John Donne, no product is an island, entire to itself. Every single product exists in a context, a large part of which is marketing. At its simplest, marketing could be defined as getting the product to its consumer. Advertising, an arm of marketing, consists of getting information about the product to the target market. Public relations, marketing's other arm, presents the product to the target market in the best possible light.

Marketing, with its appendages of advertising and public relations, is an area in which OPS can be highly effective. In any instance when a product is affected by behavior patterns, OPS can produce phenomenal results. To illustrate, this chapter shows how OPS changed my own approaches to marketing, turning a good marketing approach into a highly successful one. Then we'll turn to the daily schedules of three people, and show how the OPS program greatly enhanced their lives.

The first of these people is a marketing director for a construction/leasing/ management corporation. His story shows how OPS can best be used by those in the overall marketing field. The second is the owner of a successful full-service advertising agency, who has been on the OPS program for a year and has fine-tuned its use. The third, an executive account representative in a small, well-established public relations agency, presents some challenges for the OPS system to meet and overcome.

Recently in a Barron's publication, I read that over 30 percent of employed people have jobs directly or indirectly related to marketing functions. A whopping 45 percent of family expenditures go toward services—health care, education, recreation, professional. All in all, more than fifty cents of every dollar supports advertising, personal selling, retailing, packaging and transportation.

Because my companies represent both services and manufactured products, these statistics are very useful to my strategic planning. The four "P's" of marketing—product, price, promotion and place—are weighted heavily on promotion, both direct and indirect. Over 50 percent of my employees are involved in direct marketing, which for me is sales. But we also depend strongly on the family's decision to purchase our services, and to that end, we spend a healthy amount each year on indirect marketing efforts as well.

Many of the reports I read also analyze marketing trends, always emphasizing the importance of *why* people buy. For many years, I tried to stay in front of my markets by trying to outguess consumer behavior. Since my discovery of OPS, I have changed my view of consumer buying patterns: It may not be as important *why* people buy—it's *when.* OPS does a better job of predicting that than any other method or system I have ever found.

The obvious importance of marketing to business is mirrored in the applications of OPS to marketing. OPS can revolutionize the way some segments of marketing are undertaken. In its most specific applications, OPS performs at its peak in the area of indirect promotion—advertising and public relations.

In my experience, OPS has the potential to change the basic philosophy of media buying. Rather than purchasing time on the most popular shows across the board, choose your air time according to the OPS cycles. The most popular shows will bring gangbuster responses in Optimum Gold periods because your advertising time coincides with the time people are most likely to listen. Great results can be had during Optimum Gold times even on moderate share shows. Conversely, ads aired on the most popular shows during Fair Red period will most likely not have the same pull found during better circadian time segments.

Media buys on overnight channels, shopping networks and prime time can achieve measurable results with OPS. Forecasting market opportunities can become amazingly accurate when OPS is added to the marketing mix. Hourly, daily, weekly and monthly trends can easily be forecasted, honing market analysts' skills to a fine point. Even focus groups can be scheduled to produce optimum results. Planned product introduction can be scheduled for distribution channels most impacted by OPS. Special events also have great OPS possibilities.

The application of OPS to my own marketing program illustrates how I successfully put these ideas into effect.

OPS: Taylor's Marketing Advantage

In my own companies, marketing has always been a centerpiece in my objectives for success. One of my companies uses a market-driven manufactured product with a strong customer service component. To decide how to market this product most successfully, we looked to the scholar Philip Kotler. Kotler identified eight "demand" states that we must respond to when planning strategies. Two types of demand my company deals with are *latent* and *irregular*, as defined by Kotler. He says *latent* demand is characterized by prospective customers sharing a strong desire for satisfaction from a product that exists but doesn't satisfy. In my businesses, this means we must stay ahead of competition by doing a better job with better products. *Irregular* demands, says Kotler, occur where seasonal, daily or even hourly demand fluctuations cause major differences in product usage. For us, this means we market according to seasonal variation. Our direct marketing is done on hourly variance—although Kotler didn't know about OPS when he wrote about demand states and had no idea how right he was!

It is, therefore, my marketing manager's job to identify the latent and irregular markets and inform them of our services and manufactured products. When demand is low, we must fight to create it; in those times, marketing is our greatest ally. Our objective has always been to meet the demand with the best products and services, even when we have to pump up that demand. But we have never dictated what we think people need. We have always maintained that the purpose of business is to sell something people want, not develop something that might sell.

This philosophy has not always been subscribed to in American businesses. Historically, marketing has evolved through three phases: first, self-sufficiency; next, a sales philosophy in which a product was created and then demand was invented for it; and then to what has been called by some the "societal marketing philosophy." This theory, a step beyond the "customer knows best" way of thinking, balances the buyer, the seller and society as a whole. It works to identify the needs of consumers and satisfy those needs with a product of value to society. In my business, my goal is to sell products which are environmentally friendly (for the good of society) as well as profitable for my company. I like the societal marketing philosophy because of its good-for-people component and because it recognizes and capitalizes on a market-driven economy.

Before OPS was added to my marketing philosophy as the key to prioritizing timing, we had difficulty understanding how our customers were motivated to buy. I knew we had the right theory, but its applications didn't meet expectations in terms of response to our promotions. When we added OPS to the marketing mix, everything fell into place.

I approach marketing with the knowledge that no product sells itself. It takes creative marketing, in which OPS has proven itself again and again. I have achieved success because I have confined my marketing program to the applications in which OPS works, and not to areas in which I have no control over response.

My marketing manager has the following objectives:

1. **Analyze** the competition and find target niches of demand.
2. **Plan** strategies to develop long- and short-term opportunities to cultivate the market.

3. **Implement** activities that will achieve sales goals, using OPS to enhance the chances of succeeding.
4. **Control**, **measure** and **monitor** the results and go back to step one if results fall short.

Step three, implementation, embraces one area of marketing—promotion, and uses two methods—direct and indirect. Chapter 3 concerns itself with direct promotion, which is personal sales. Indirect promotion in my business covers these areas: radio ads, television ads and promotional events. Later in this chapter I will discuss additional marketing methods made effective by the use of OPS, but for my business, radio, TV and promotions are the most effective methods of indirect marketing.

To elaborate on the idea I spoke about in chapter three, radio has proven to be my greatest marketing resource. I can measure the success of using celebrity endorsers, who talk about my company and its products, in a time slot chosen according to OPS. Previous attempts at image-oriented promotions proved vague and the results were unmeasurable. Because I can control the airwaves, at least through my spokespeople, OPS has provided me with enhanced sales.

How do I achieve this? I only buy air time in Optimum Gold, Excellent Green and Moderate Blue time segments. People call the office after they hear my advertisements. Because of my historical and ongoing statistical studies I am convinced that they call because they not only *heard* the ad, but *listened* to it. In my studies, Fair Red times, which sometimes encompass as much as 35 percent of the workday, simply did not pull response. From experience with OPS, we know that people are more willing to listen and buy during the more intense OPS times rather than the less intense Fair Red segments. These Fair Red times, varying in length from one to three hours, always divide Optimum Gold, Excellent Green and Moderate Blue from each other. Response in these times was significantly lower, about the same as sales percentages (see the chart in chapter 3).

Now I have an excellent product, competitively priced, and targeted through the right channels for promotion. The message design appeals to my spokespeople's audiences, the message structure focuses on benefits, and the message format reflects my highly credible spokesperson. In other words, the advertisements are quite typical for radio advertising. They share the same elements as successful advertisements all over the world.

The difference in success rate rests in OPS.

My company's television time is bringing in results similar to those of radio time. I know that choosing air time during Optimum Gold segments substantially improves my chances of closing a sale. My options range from traditional network advertising to home shopping networks to infomercials. I have produced advertisements in each of these media and have instructed my marketing people to buy time *only* in accordance with the OPS calendar. My goal is to attract every insomniac homeowner during the midnight Optimum Golds!

Because I am constantly investigating new channels for my marketing information, I am presently considering the use of E-Mail. On-line services such as Prodigy, CompuServe, America Online and Delphi Internet will soon be joined by Microsoft, Apple, AT&T and Ziff-Davis in cyberspace. Some of these on-line services project having up to 20 million subscribers by the turn of the century. If I can use my OPS media-buying calendar on the information superhighway, my company has a good chance of beating the competition in any lane.

For me, using OPS to determine marketing channels has had three important results: OPS has extended my reach, reduced the number of ads required and maximized the impact of each ad that airs.

The Many Hats of Lewis Kinney

In a family business such as the one owned by the Kinneys, operations don't have the same impersonal, "strictly business" stance seen in many corporations. In this particular case, the business was begun before World War II by Lewis's father who, at nearly 80 years of age, still comes to work every day, imprinting his style on the company. Many employees have been with the company for over 30 years, though a younger set has made some recent changes in the way the company is run.

Originally, the company built private residences, developing whole neighborhoods in a growing Michigan city after the war. During the 1950s, the boom for houses slackened, and Lewis's father turned to building warehouses. He had a keen eye for which part of the city would become commercial, and he was one of the first to build warehouses on speculation, shelling the exterior and fitting the interiors to custom order when the building was leased. The family, which included Lewis's many uncles, all of whom worked for the company at one time or another, built and leased most of the warehouse space in this burgeoning city for over 40 years.

The city's growth slowed in the 1980s, and the construction business plummeted nationally as well as locally. By the late 1980s, after Lewis had been with the company for about seven years, he was intimately familiar with the company's long history. In fact, he had been convinced until his early teens that his father had built the entire city, an opinion not far off the fact. His father was indeed a major figure in the construction landscape of the city. Everybody knew, had heard of, or leased property from Lewis's family. But during the 1980s, new companies came in from faraway states. Business began to take on a different coloration from the handshake attitude that originally built and maintained the company. It was time for a different approach to marketing and perhaps a rethinking of the company's entire structure.

Lewis was the younger of two brothers responsible for the company's daily operations. He managed the marketing side, and was involved in both direct and indirect promotion. He played a major part in the company's evolution in the last five years as its focus shifted almost entirely to the leasing and lease management aspect of the business. This shift resulted in the narrowing of marketing channels for the company. Although accustomed to placing construction advertisements in trade journals, Lewis realized the consumers he reached had not been the company's target market for several years. At this point, Lewis switched to commercial real estate brokers and word of mouth as his primary marketing tools. These methods have been remarkably successful for the company, which has enjoyed a superior reputation in the community.

Today, however, Lewis's company must compete with the city's other lease/management companies. In addition, the company owns the majority of the properties they lease and, since many of those properties are approaching the half-century mark, capital improvements are becoming part of the leasing agreements. In order to compete, the company must offer special incentives in an increasingly difficult market.

Lewis is looking for an advantage that will provide him with the best opportunity to sell a potential client his company's services. Combating aging space and a target client base that may never have heard of his company, Lewis decided to see if OPS couldn't provide the edge his business needed. He shared with us a typical workday, and asked us to reschedule it with the following priorities:

1. Appointment to lease space.
2. Meeting with a property manager to check on problems with physical damages or other tenant problems.
3. Work on lease renewals.
4. Create sales letters and proposals.

Since Lewis is largely responsible for scheduling his own day, his routine begins at 8:30 a.m. He will compose and dictate letters until about 10:30 a.m., when he likes to get out of the office for site visitations before lunch. He frequently has lunch out of the office with members of his network, and tries to schedule afternoon site visitations after lunch, arriving back at the office around 2:30 p.m. Lewis spends the rest of the afternoon making sure at least one leasing agent—there are three, including himself—is in the office to answer the telephone. As a general rule, afternoons are spent drafting proposals for new business, taking telephone calls from the many properties the company manages and preparing for sales presentations.

We asked Lewis to reconsider his routine to take advantage of OPS. He is fortunate enough to have a secretary who can field his calls so that he can return them in the most favorable OPS time.

Lewis Kinney's OPS Day

8:00 a.m. Fair Red	Arrive at office. Dictate sales letters and develop sales proposals for new business.
9:00-9:30 a.m. Fair Red Optimum Gold to 10:00 a.m.	Travel to on-site sales appointment. Meet with potential tenants. Every effort is made to close deal.
10:00 a.m. Optimum Gold	Another on-site meeting with potential clients.
11:00 a.m. Optimum Gold	Meet at another property about leaky roof and collection problem with tenant. Defer decision about collection until later in the afternoon, as tenant is too crisis-driven to be reasonable.
12:00 noon Optimum Gold	Lunch with bankers to discuss capital improvement campaign. Get commitment for resources by the end of lunch.
1:00 p.m. Optimum Gold	Lease renewal meetings. Close before 2:30 p.m., when time sequence shifts to Fair Red.
2:00 p.m. Optimum Gold to 2:30 p.m.\Fair Red to 3:00 p.m.	Return to office, get messages, and return phone calls not having to do with lease closings. If unavoidable, reschedule calls on closings for a more auspicious time.
3:00 p.m. Fair Red	Write thank-you and follow-up letters, and write reports for morning and noon meetings. Contact tenant regarding collection problem.

4:00 p.m. Moderate Blue	Design new marketing piece for corporate relocation target market. Make and return phone calls to potential clients. Check Optimum Gold and Excellent Green times for next few days, then make appointments with qualifying clients to view properties.
5:00 p.m. Moderate Blue	Make networking phone calls to brokers for new business. Meet with brother to strategize meetings with potential clients.
6:00 p.m. Moderate Blue	Leave office.

Lewis carefully followed the OPStime calendar, making sure that he was meeting with all decision makers and closing all sales before the time shifted to Fair Red. He began traveling to other cities to meet with potential relocating corporations, adjusting his personal clock to their OPS times. He could then manage when his presentation materials were read and could make himself available to answer questions. When the potential clients came to his city, he could schedule them in an OPS time favorable to *them*, even though they were in his time zone because their biological clocks would only adjust at the rate of two hours per day—not enough to matter on the usual whirlwind tour.

In less than three weeks, Lewis began to notice that time prioritizing by OPS was paying off in more closings on new leases and renewals.

Ad Energy Marketing Group

Spencer Lawson heads up a full-service advertising agency in Arizona. He is very busy these days because of the flight of earthquake-anxious

Californians into his state. They buy his primary client's automotive products, which in turn drives his agency to overtime.

It would appear that Spencer has always worked overtime. Among his friends and clients, he has a reputation as a man who will work all night to wrestle a marketing problem to the ground. Perhaps it is this reputation that has made his agency more successful than ever in the last year. Or it could be the influx of population. Spencer, however, knows it is neither. But he keeps the real reasons to himself. He likes the edge he has on his competition, so he guards his secret.

Spencer became intrigued by the idea of circadian rhythms, knowing deep down that the shifting and moving of the time segments was important. When he began using the program, he quickly realized that the time segments were what he had been experiencing as "feelings" for many years. Sensitive to nuance, pattern and seasonal cycles, Spencer immediately put OPS into his life, both personally and professionally. He describes himself as a person whose attitude and outlook run very close to OPS; they did that long before we ever discovered it, he says. "I could always get myself up to 50 percent speed," he says. "But sometimes I could rev up to 90 percent. Today I know that 90 percent is pure OPS Gold."

Because he owns his own business in a service area, Spencer is able to call the shots on his schedule. His application of OPS is somewhat unusual, but it does illustrate how Spencer pulls the most productive times out of a 24-hour time period. He considers the telephone a deadly weapon, and instructs his staff on a daily basis about the OPS hours in which he will take and make calls. With the telephone managed, he is then able to carve two regular workdays out of his regular OPS schedule. He finds himself as effective at night during Optimum Gold and Excellent Green levels of the rhythms, so he schedules a nap every day during the red times. To him, night is like a second day.

When he plans his week, he initially structures it to the times when he must "interface with the world," as he puts it — the basic 9:00 a.m. to 5:00 p.m. He plans according to his priorities matched to OPS. He has four priorities: what he calls "creative engineering"; cost effectiveness projects; client relations; and creative production. To show how Spencer arranges his two workdays in one, we have chosen to illustrate one of his 24-hour plans.

Spencer Lawson's Circadian Day

8:00 a.m. to 9:30 a.m. Fair Red\9:30 a.m. to 12:00 noon Optimum Gold	Having worked until 2:30 a.m. to take advantage of an overnight Optimum Gold, Spencer sleeps for six hours, rising about 8:30 a.m. He arrives at his office by 9:30 a.m. and immediately dives into a client relations project, a top business priority perfectly suited to Optimum Gold time.
12:00 noon Optimum Gold	Creative production time, used to invent the advertisements that will do his clients the most good.
1:00 p.m. to 2:30 p.m. Optimum Gold	Lunch with client. Spencer considers himself as much a part of his clients' businesses as his own, thus a midday Optimum Gold period is always reserved for meeting with clients, even when no project is due. It is an excellent time to forge deeper relationships.
2:30 p.m. Fair Red	Spencer returns to his office, where he takes care of filing and paperwork.
4:00 p.m. to 6:00 p.m. Moderate Blue	Cost effectiveness analysis is Spencer's Blue period priority. Client by client he reviews the resources spent on each, and explores how they

	can be used more efficiently. He also uses this time to finalize creative projects. He reserves his major creative production work for the more intense Excellent Green or Optimum Gold times.
7:00 p.m. to 9:00 p.m. Fair Red	Spencer returns home for a 90-minute nap. Then he gets up and eats a good supper high in carbohydrates to help him through the marathon creative time approaching at 10:00 p.m.
10:00 p.m. to 2:00 a.m. Optimum Gold	This is Spencer's time to do creative engineering, which he defines as studying the client's whole business and looking at it with fresh eyes. He uses this time away from intrusions to do research, read publications and examine the approaches the agency and clients are using. Every possible thing that impacts marketing for clients is reassessed by Spencer during these middle-of-the-night sessions.
3:00 a.m. to 4:30 a.m. Fair Red	Spencer may eat a light meal before going to sleep until 9:00 a.m. He takes advantage of 90-minute sleep cycles to catch a six-hour sleep.

You might want to know how Spencer handles the nitty-gritty details and minute-by-minute crises that often occur in the advertising business. His activity level during the Optimum Gold time in the middle of this particular day is very high; his staff knows they can reach him by cel-phone at any time, and they know what to bother him with in a client meeting and what to handle themselves. Spencer has taught them how to prioritize emergencies according to OPS, and this lesson has smoothed out operations considerably. Also, Spencer has deliberately removed himself from the minute details that plague many executives. He realizes that his clients are paying him to think, not to implement—his staff is highly trained for that function. Finally, Spencer is very self-motivated and disciplined. Not many people would be willing to put in another whole day beginning at 10:00 p.m., or wake up at 2:00 a.m. to catch the Optimum Gold period swinging through the night. OPS has given him an organized structure to hang his priorities upon, and he has used it to optimum advantage. After all, he wants to live up to his reputation.

Public Relations Challenges

Sandra Myers is a senior account executive for a small, well-established public relations agency in a midwestern city. Married, but without children, she is building her career and thus willing to spend long days at the office. Second in command behind the agency's owner, she supervises all agency accounts and a staff of four, excluding a fairly constant supply of interns from local academic institutions. She handles five accounts exclusively. Her average day always includes writing press releases for her accounts, proofreading, reviewing and revising all the others' work. She writes memos, publicity summaries and status reports for her accounts and oversees everyone else's. She also prepares sales and position papers as well as functioning as new business person.

She observes that on her average days, she tries to be proactive, but finds that reactive behavior takes 50 percent of her time—and she says she had to fight like hell to get that far. On bad days, which are approximately two and a half days per week, she finds herself being 100 percent reactive. Her crises usually originate with clients or with her boss, who fails to recognize Sandra's attempts to gain control over her schedule. Sandra characterizes her boss as a 110 percent reactive person who laterals her own crisis situations to her staff. In addition, increasing the difficulty of her average days, Sandra also spends most or all of some days conducting media tours on the properties of several clients. And to top off everything else, one major client, which pays a large retainer, expects full-time attention and often demands four to five times as much work from Sandra as it pays for.

Sandra's goals include doing more market research and getting a broader range of clients to whom she could offer even more services than the agency currently provides. She would like to spend more time honing presentation skills for new sales, but does not want her accessibility to clients diminished, since access and personal service are two of the primary marketing tools this agency uses.

How can OPS help Sandra take control of her day and still remain accessible? Recognizing that Sandra has some daunting challenges, we first let her know that it takes a lot of courage to change even the things one can, and that a time-prioritizing system takes some time to work out. Given her pressure-cooker situation, we recommended that she take charge of one time segment at a time. By increasing her time management a bit each day, she will soon experience control over her entire schedule.

The following chart reports an average day for Sandra. Notice how it is broken into small fragments, often taking as little as 15 minutes for work that under ordinary circumstances should take an hour—or taking an hour for something that could take 15 minutes. She had planned in advance her interview with the freelance writer, the photo shoot, the 4:00 p.m. new client meeting, the focus group, and the client dinner. The hotel press release was also on her planned agenda. Lunch with her boss was spontaneously arranged by her boss 15 minutes prior.

A Non-OPS Day for Sandra Myers

8:00 a.m.	Arrive at office. Make phone calls about mailer for hotel client. Phone meeting with hotel client. Meet with boss.
9:00 a.m.	Revise press releases. Phone meeting about planning special

	events for upcoming holiday. Revise press releases from other staff.
10:00 a.m.	Meet with freelance writer doing a story on hotel client. Supervise photo shoot.
11:00 a.m. to 11:30 a.m.	Do invitations for client dinner and prepare media list for same. Leave phone message for financial client.
12:00 noon	Finalize press release for hotel with client. Go to lunch with boss to discuss new business strategies.
1:00 p.m.	Review client dinner press release. Write thank-you letters to media tour participants. Revise conference meeting minutes. Leave messages with clients and handle production details for print order.
2:00 p.m.	Do client status reports, media relations trip itinerary, and research for special event.
3:00 p.m.	Write new business proposals and sales letters.
4:00 p.m.	Meet with new client to plan media presentations, press materials, and other story ideas.
5:00 p.m.	Work on media list for new client. Coordinate newsletter labels for another client, return phone calls and confirm focus group.
6:00 p.m.	Attend focus group and meet clients for dinner.
8:00 p.m.	Go home.

Sandra made a list of the things over which she had no control and those she did. We analyzed it together and found that the no-control issues actually boiled down to two: the phone and her boss. Although she says she is functionally incapable of ignoring a ringing phone, for the purposes of OPS time prioritizing, we recommended Sandra rethink her need to answer all calls. On the other hand, she has no choice but to accept and work with her boss's tendency to interrupt. OPS proved helpful in dealing with both the phone and her boss.

We randomly selected a day in early fall for rearranging Sandra's schedule by OPS priority. Her long day possessed all four circadian time segments for her to use advantageously.

An OPS Day for Sandra Myers

8:00 a.m. Excellent Green	Meet for 30 minutes with freelance writer doing story on hotel client. Meet with boss and give her the day's agenda.
9:00 a.m. Fair Red	Move photo shoot and revise press releases for self and staff. Call about mailer.
10:00 a.m. to 10:30 a.m. Fair Red	Do invitations and media list.
10:30 a.m. to 12:00 noon Moderate Blue	Write new business proposals and sales letters. Conduct phone meeting for special events planning. Make phone calls and leave messages; make arrangements to avoid taking calls between 1:30 p.m. and 4:30 p.m.
12:00 noon Moderate Blue	Talk to boss about new business strategies, as this is the best OPS time for creative and objective thinking. Keep it down to one hour.

1:00 p.m. to 1:30 p.m. Moderate Blue	Review client dinner press release.
1:30 p.m. to 2:00 p.m. Fair Red	Write client status reports, trip itinerary, and thank-you letters. Finalize hotel press release. Revise conference meeting minutes.
2:00 p.m. Fair Red	Work on media list for new client and coordinate newsletter labels for another client. Return phone calls and confirm focus group.
3:00 p.m. to 4:30 p.m. Fair Red	Focus on production details, research project and new market research.
4:30 p.m. to 6:00 p.m. Optimum Gold	Meet with new client to plan media presentations, press materials and other story ideas.
6:00 p.m. to 8:00 p.m. Optimum Gold	Attend focus group and have dinner with clients. This is the best OPS time for both of these functions.
8:00 p.m. Optimum Gold	Go home.

By rearranging Sandra's schedule according to OPS priority times, we were able to accomplish a number of objectives:

* Administrative and busy work were all lumped together in Fair Red

times to take advantage of less intense circadian time.

* By presenting her agenda to her boss in the early morning, Sandra deflected her boss's tendency to interrupt, at least in part.

* Sandra requested that the agency's receptionist ask each caller if he could have his call returned between 1:30 p.m. and 4:30 p.m. If the caller said that a crisis was in progress, the receptionist could tell the caller that the call would be reported to Sandra "as soon as she is out of her meeting." That way, Sandra could decide the priority of the crisis and deal with it accordingly.

* At lunch, she was able to report on new business letters she had already completed, and all of her phone calls were returned in a timely fashion.

* We were able to find an entire hour out of Sandra's already overburdened schedule to conduct new market research simply by arranging her priorities to OPS.

SIX

WHAT'S OPS, DOC?

Medicine and Psychiatry Come in on Time

Dear Bob,

As a specialist in pediatric and adolescent medicine, I have always held a profound respect for the intricate workings of my patients' inner clocks, as well as my own. In fact, my partner and I tried for many months to figure out a way to work and feel better. We tried everything from changing our diets to changing the times we ate to starting various exercise programs. I even tried hypnosis. Nothing worked.

The more I experienced, and the more I studied, the evidence of some great pattern connecting the ticking of all the clocks became overwhelming. And like you, for many years I could not figure out what the pattern was. Now you have cracked the code. When I received the OPS program, I said, "No wonder nothing else we tried worked!"

The potential OPS applications to the practice of medicine are only a beginning. It might be even possible to consider many disease states as out-of-phase biological clocks. I firmly believe you have developed an incredible program that will work for everyone. And the best part is that it is not based on anything magical or mystical. I am with you all the way to put these great insights into clinical practice.

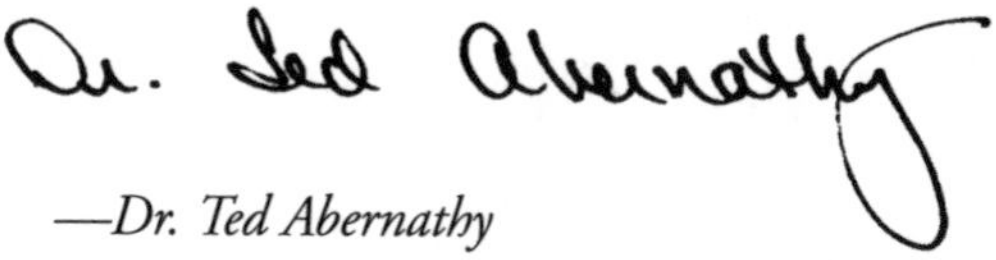

—Dr. Ted Abernathy

To the medical and psychiatric professions, knowledge of how this master clock ticks could help in the treatment of many physical and mental diseases. In hospitals and emergency rooms, knowledge of OPS could increase the chances of survival for patients by working *with* the biological clocks rather than against them. Plus, hospital staffing administrators could predict peak patient flows with more reasonable certainty.

Dr. Abernathy's experience with putting OPS into practice illustrates how one physician has been able to implement the circadian calendar.

Now that we have established the code patterns for the circadian rhythms through OPS, Dr. Abernathy and his colleagues can take our circadian calendar and work with their schedules and patients on an individual basis. In this chapter, we will explore the potentials for OPS in some major medical and psychiatric areas currently under the microscope of the pioneering chronobiologists. We have made some inroads with our research into applications of OPS to these areas, but it is our intent to raise more questions than answers in this chapter. As with any exciting new field, the possibilities are thrilling. It is as if we were botanists discovering a whole valley full of flowers no one has ever seen or described. All we know is that they are flowers; it is our job to catalog, to test, to figure out how they fit into the rest of the world.

In his city, Dr. Abernathy chairs the pediatrics department at one hospital and sits on the board of another. Several of his colleagues do the same. Both hospitals hold monthly board meetings, usually on Wednesdays. Dr. Abernathy and his partner have control over the agenda of one hospital's meeting, but no control over the other. For the last seven months, Dr. Abernathy planned his meeting agenda according to the OPS time segment in which the meeting has been scheduled. His criteria for adjusting the agenda is taken from the "What's Hot/What's Not" charts beginning on page 26 in chapter 2. If the meeting is scheduled during an Excellent Green or Moderate Blue period, the doctor will bring up and discuss important issues such as buying a major new piece of equipment or deciding critical policy issues. If he wants to convince his board to take action on something, he will wait for a meeting held during Optimum Gold. If he wants to hold a roundtable discussion on creative ways to run the hospital better, he holds out for a Moderate Blue time. In Fair Red times, he schedules only routine matters. He makes no attempt to accomplish goals mismatched to their respective time segments.

Over the months, Dr. Abernathy has noticed that the meetings in which he has applied OPS have been productive and calm. The other hospital, however, conducts meetings in the same way they have for many years, with the same high level of frustration and inability to get anything concrete done. The interesting thing to Dr. Abernathy is that both meetings used to be exactly the same!

"I know we have successful meetings and a very successful hospital," he says. "The other hospital is set up basically in the same way and operated just the way it always has been. Other doctors we know still have the same frustrating meetings, and we don't anymore. Our results have changed." For Dr. Abernathy, operating on OPS has greatly enhanced his work and his hospital.

Time for Medicine

Chronobiology, once on the edges of science, is gaining wider acceptance in the scientific community. Once, the theories about biological clocks were considered to have no practical application, but today's discoveries are changing the way medical therapies are administered. OPS, reflecting the intensity levels of the circadian rhythms, could have dramatic impact on the times some of these treatments should be administered.

In the following sections, we'll explore some of the fascinating discoveries and possible applications of OPS.

Babies

At 1:30 a.m. on a Thursday morning in June 1985, a big city hospital pediatric wing was in a controlled panic. Three out of five birthing rooms were occupied, and each of the three women in them was about to deliver. One had been in labor for 22 hours, another for three and the third had come in 30 minutes earlier. With only one doctor on the floor, the staff was stretched to its capacity. All three babies came within 20 minutes of each other; the doctor was present at the pushing stage of labor for two of them. Frantic calls to another pediatrician had produced a sleepy intern who supervised the third delivery along with a midwife who just happened to be in the hospital emergency room with an asthmatic child.

All the babies and mothers were fine. The staff, however, could have used a vacation. Fortunately, none of the deliveries presented any complications, though statistically fewer problems arise in births born at that hour.

Unfortunately, all this occurred before OPS was developed. Had the Optimum Performance Schedule been around, the hospital would have known this night would contain an Optimum Gold period that would peak around 1:30 a.m. Statistics show that most women go into labor between 1:30 a.m. and 2:30 a.m. Add an Optimum Gold time to that fact, and the chances are excellent that the pediatric wings of any given hospital will be lively at that hour. An extra doctor, midwife and nurse or two should have been on call or on the floor, and the births might have been handled more smoothly.

To test our idea that babies like to be born during the most intense times of the circadian rhythms, we gathered birth times data from the state of Georgia over a two-year period. In our preliminary study, we found that slightly more babies were born during Optimum Gold and Excellent

Percent Deviation of Births Occurring in Each OPS Time Relative to the Baseline Average of 11.96 Births Per Hour

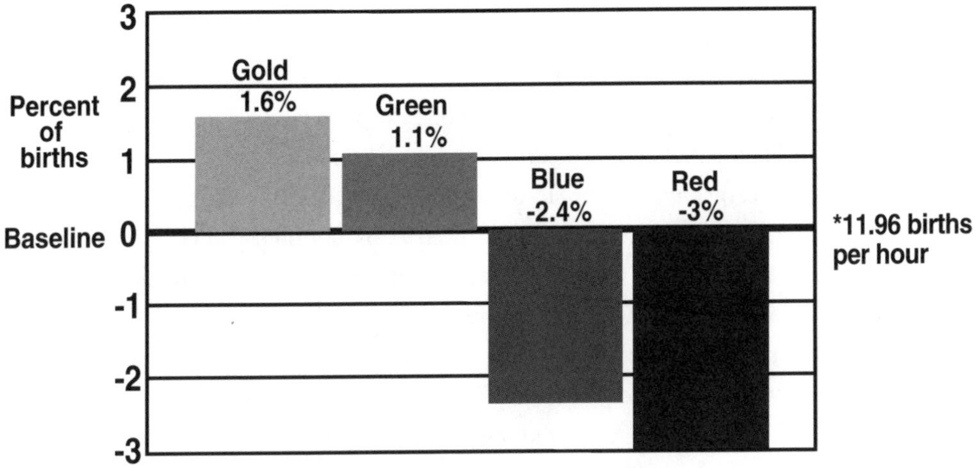
3
2
1
0
-1
-2
-3
Percent of births
Baseline
Gold 1.6%
Green 1.1%
Blue -2.4%
Red -3%
*11.96 births per hour

Study sample taken 1992-1993, state of Georgia

Going for the Gold and Green . . .

In a more than two-year study across Georgia, we found that more babies arrived within the gold and green time segments than during the blue and red. Considering that blue and red periods comprise most of an average day, our results demonstrate a practical significance for hospitals working on staffing schedules. It would be advisable to increase staffing during gold and green time segments.

Green times (see chart above). Considering that Moderate Blue and Fair Red times comprise over 50 percent of the average 24-hour period, hospitals would be well advised to check staff resources and adjust for those times.

OPS charts the circadian day around the clock, but as everybody knows, babies like to be born at night. Optimum Gold and Excellent Green time segments rotate through the hours of darkness just as they do through daylight. We are currently testing the hypothesis that the nighttime circadian segments behave differently than their daylight partners with respect to labor and delivery.

We do not believe there is any difference in the general intensity of nighttime and daytime segments. The circadian rhythms themselves are not the factor for nighttime births. There are other reasons why babies enter the world during the dark. Some theorists postulate that babies are born at night because our early ancestors would usually find a safe place to stay then. In a basically nomadic existence in which the tribe is hunting, gathering and moving during the day, giving birth was a function that could slow down and in some cases endanger the community. Even today, midday labors are least frequent, and statistics show that births between 2:00 p.m. and 4:00 p.m. have a greater chance for complications in both mother and child.

When OPS is coordinated with known factors for births, the chances of predicting peak delivery times are greatly enhanced. We look forward to sharing our knowledge with interested medical personnel in this area, and actively solicit medical records for testing our statistical results.

Premenstrual Syndrome

On a clear winter's day at the Hast Publishing Company, Dana Parsons sat on a low bench in the ladies' restroom. The bench, between a shower stall and the wall, remained hidden from view unless the very last stall was in use. This was the most secluded spot in the entire company except for the private offices enjoyed by senior editors and advertising people. Dana's work station afforded her no privacy, so she came here to cry.

An editor offered her some mild criticism about one of her graphic layouts, and Dana overreacted, becoming quite defensive and walking off in a huff. In the restroom, she sat alone, in tears, and waited for this terrible mood to pass.

It's "just PMS."

If women (and their husbands, children and bosses) could schedule PMS days, the world might be more tolerant of this controversial medical condition. It is controversial because some people still can't believe that hormones can exact as big a toll on behavior as PMS appears to. But for about 10 percent of women, PMS is severe enough to be called "depression on schedule." Irritability, fatigue, aches, pains and tears at the drop of a hat drive both victims and people around them to distraction. Productive work time is lost, marital battles are most intense and children are wrongly sent to their rooms without supper. But recent research has revealed some startling conclusions about PMS, and we would like to add OPS to the mix in understanding how and when this condition is at its most intense.

PMS is worse in winter, when the circadian rhythms are the least intense and immune systems are weakest. Studies have shown that women who suffer the most from PMS have the least amount of the "sleep-time" hormone, melatonin, as well as the "rise and shine" hormone, serotonin, in their bloodstreams during winter months. Therefore the rise and fall of the hormones in their bloodstream cycled faster than normally.

A study concerning PMS was conducted in which victims skipped a night's sleep in order to restart their cycle. This is a technique now being used with depression, too, and researchers figured it was worth a try. It worked. Eight out of 10 women included in the study improved.

If light cycles influence hormones, as this and other studies are showing, how do the circadian rhythms impact them? Could Optimum Gold and Excellent Green times possibly intensify the symptoms of PMS? We do know that the more intense the time period, the more intense the behavior—and that includes positive as well as negative behavior. With OPS, women and others concerned with PMS can check the premenstrual cycle far in advance to see where Optimum Gold and Excellent Green times dominate. During the winter, knowing these times may help women like Dana schedule medication dosages and daily agendas to account for PMS. And in the years to come, OPS could help physicians schedule light cures along with hormone medications.

Anesthesia

Anesthesiologists and chronobiologists may have many interesting things to share with each other. Anesthesiologists already know that seasonal and annual rhythms affect the potency of the chemicals they use to put people under during surgery. Animal studies have shown that more medication is needed at times the animal is most active, which for most animals is during the day. The daily rise and fall of hormones in humans could also affect anesthesia, just as age, weight, height, drug sensitivity and medical condition do. In addition, the time segments shifting through the circadian day could influence the potency of anesthesia. Could Fair Red times indicate less anesthesia is needed, and Optimum Gold times the most? Should surgeries be scheduled in Optimum Gold times to assure the surgeon's peak performance, or in a Moderate Blue time to adjust to the patient's drug tolerance levels? These are only a few of the intriguing questions the professionals in each field need to be discussing.

Cancer

One of our most touching and dramatic stories came to us from a doctor whose wife is suffering from cancer. Diagnosed a number of years ago with colon cancer, she underwent the accustomed round of surgery and chemotherapy. Last year, she developed a particularly rapid-spreading type of ovarian cancer. She began another round of chemotherapy in the hopes that it would stop the growth and kill the cancer cells.

She used a particular type of chemotherapy in which the medicine was given to her through an IV continuously for 23 hours, building up the dose over time. Her husband, using the OPS calendar, arranged for her chemotherapy to be given to her only on OPS days favorable for success. He used the schedule to find days in which two Optimum Gold time segments appeared, preferably one beginning in the very early morning (such as 2:00 a.m.), and the other beginning in the afternoon, when the dosage would be at its peak.

Last October, her doctors decided to operate, though they were not hopeful about the results. The cancer mass appeared to be invading the intestine, and they needed to find out how far it extended and remove as much as possible.

To their delight and surprise, they found that the mass had separated from the intestinal wall, and appeared encapsulated (not to have spread). They removed the mass, and put her on a clean-up dose of chemotherapy, which she still takes according to OPS.

There are several miracles in this story. She had not become sick from the chemotherapy ever since being put on an OPS schedule—a distinct change from her previous experience. Second, the ovarian cancer should have killed her. It didn't. She beat the odds.

How much credit can OPS take for this? We don't know. It is only one story, and there are millions more out there. We do know that chemotherapy works by killing cells at certain stages of their life cycles. It would stand to reason that those cycles are influenced by the circadian as well as the infradian and ultradian clocks. We believe that the chances are good that the doctor and his wife were working with the biological clocks rather than against them.

Cancer is complex, coming in many forms and with many treatments. Incredible strides have been made in its treatment, but no cure-all has been found. Many treatments are considered controversial, some merely idiosyncratic. But chronobiology offers some potentially wonderful solutions to certain problems of timing. Some examples:

* One study found that women who had breast cancer surgery right after ovulation quadrupled their chances of living cancer-free for 10 years. Is this the influence of infradian time? Researchers have not nailed the answers down, but some physicians are coordinating surgery with menstrual cycles.

* Other studies show that the temperatures of tumors rise and fall; when treated at the height of this cycle, some tumors shrank 40 percent more than those treated at other times.

* "Best" times have been documented for over 20 anticancer drugs. They take into account the body's rhythms, hormonal levels at particular times of day, temperature cycles and even annual cycles in the immune system.

* Researchers have been able to lower toxicity of drug treatments in animals with leukemia by varying dosages according to the circadian rhythms.

* Kidney toxicity from the drug cisplatin in patients with advanced cancer can be lowered by varying doses with the time of day.

* Human bone toxicity from adriamycin can apparently be reduced by dosing according to circadian rhythms.

The prospects for integrating OPS with the areas chronobiologists are studying are exciting. We truly believe that miracle stories such as that of the doctor and his wife will become everyday occurrences as this work continues.

Heart Disease

Perhaps no part of the human body gets more attention for its rhythms than the heart. Indeed, it deserves this focus; without it, studies of other rhythms wouldn't make much sense.

Research has turned up some interesting facts about the cycles affecting the heart. Need we say, circadian rhythms may be among the most significant? Some examples:

* Heart attacks peak in January and February, just when immune systems

—and the circadian rhythms—are at their lowest ebb. Concentrations of hormones and cholesterol are different during these times as well.

* 40 percent more heart attacks occur on Mondays than any other day. Thursdays and Saturdays are second-best (or worst) days for heart attacks. On Mondays, people who have relaxed into circadian days over the weekend must yank their schedules backward to readjust for the work week. It's like having jet lag every Monday. Coincidence? Not to a chronobiologist.

* Angina, episodes of chest pain, occur when not enough blood gets to the heart. It has a cycle, too. About 30 minutes before people rise in the morning, blood clots more easily—at the exact time our hearts can adjust least easily. So more angina occurs in the morning—and more on winter mornings than any other time of year. Do early morning OPS times influence the heart's ability to respond? Could we watch for Fair Red times as possible danger signals in angina's agenda? Studies may soon show the correlation.

* People with high blood pressure don't have it all the time. It goes up and down all day. A 15-percent spread in the diastolic reading isn't at all unusual in a healthy person. But for those whose blood pressure is chronically high, this upward spike could spell trouble. Some people spike at night. Others only spike in the doctor's office. Blood pressure, it seems, has a mind of its own. As doctors learn more about how to watch the ticking of biological clocks, it might become easier to predict how an individual's blood pressure is going to behave over time. Does a week full of Optimum Gold afternoons have an effect on blood pressure? Does it go down during Fair Red times? We shall see.

Mental OPS And Downs

"The trouble is," said the chief diagnostician, "we don't know what the trouble is. — It is impossible to tell whether the patient has clockitis, clockosis, clockoma, or clocktheria. . . . The patient may have one of the minor clock ailments . . . such as clockets, clockles, clocking cough, ticking pox, or clumps. We shall have to develop area men who will find out about such areas —"

—James Thurber, *The Thirteen Clocks*

Some "area men" are already working on what could become major breakthroughs in psychiatry. Sleep disorders and even more serious psychiatric problems such as clinical depression comprise only a few of the subjects being studied. The suffering causing untold anguish for victims and their families for thousands of years may at last be coming to an end. In their restless, unending search for answers and cures, scientists daily unlock the mysteries of our minds and the chemical intricacies that cause mental diseases. One of the fields being explored is chronobiology, and how the hundreds of biological clocks influence the brains of those afflicted with both mild and severe disorders. In having cracked the circadian code connected to a master clock, we are exploring the possibilities that OPS can help science in this great cause.

Seasonal Affective Disorder

Dan Jacobson had two professions. During six months of the year, he supervised construction crews in Minneapolis, Minnesota, and during the winter months he spent his days in the spotless garages of a luxury automobile dealer working on the insides of cars.

Bright, personable and a hard worker for most of the year, Dan's performance began to drop off every October, bottomed out around January and didn't really right itself until March. In recent years, he shortened his work schedule at the automobile dealer to accommodate what had become a serious health problem.

Dan got depressed every winter. He slept long hours, was irritable most of the time, lost interest in sex, ate more starchy foods and gained weight. His mother said he'd had most of these symptoms since childhood. His wife blamed the fact that the children were underfoot more during the winter months because they couldn't go outside. In some years, the family managed to go to the Texas coast for a week or two during February. Dan became his old self during these excursions. His lifted spirits dropped off when he'd returned home, but usually picked up again in late March, when he could get outdoors. By April, when construction picked up, Dan had become his summertime self.

Dan's wintertime employer had an employee assistance program. During a routine health screening, a nurse began to question Dan about his blue moods. She referred him to a psychiatrist, who diagnosed him with Seasonal Affective Disorder, or SAD, and began treating him with light.

With light? Dan's first reaction was skeptical. But after he sat in a phototherapy box for a few hours on successive days, exposing himself to lights that duplicate natural sunlight, he became convinced. He began going home feeling like his summertime self.

Dan didn't need just any old light. Ordinary room light is only one-twentieth the strength of daylight. Phototherapists measure light in units called a *lux*—different from the old measurements called foot candles. A bright sunlit day may produce 80,000 lux, an ordinary day about 10,000. For Dan's treatment to work, he needs about 2,500 lux, or nearly 2,000 more than room light.

But if there is such an amazing cure for SAD, why doesn't everybody know about it? In fact, it was not until 1987 that SAD was recognized by the American Psychiatric Association, though cases have been documented throughout history, especially in the northern countries of the world. It turns out that the further north one lives, the better the odds of becoming part of the 25 percent of the population at risk.

Why does light work? Apparently, that good-time, sleep-time hormone melatonin has its down side, so to speak. When we don't get enough light to generate its hormonal wide-awake partner, serotonin, melatonin just keeps on going. People with SAD have an oversupply of melatonin and an undersupply of serotonin in their bloodstreams all the time during the winter. Since these two hormones respond to light, phototherapists can treat the disorder with it. No drugs, no invasive treatments; how de*lux*e!

Because the study of SAD is still so new, scientists are uncertain how the rest of the biological clocks influence SAD. Light cures work for about 85 percent of patients, and seem to work best during morning hours. We are interested in the effects of the circadian clocks on these treatments. Is there an OPS time segment that would lessen treatment duration? Would light cures work better in Fair Red time segments, when patients are experiencing the least intensity of the circadian day? Some patients complain that too much light makes them hyperactive and wide awake at night. Would a combination of changing the OPS time with reducing length of treatment work best for them? Would the 15 percent who do not respond well to light therapy perhaps be helped by timing the treatments to individual clocks combined with OPS?

Look for answers coming to light within the next two years.

Depression

Judy Neal, an ordinary housewife and mother, began to behave strangely in her forty-second year. Sometimes she would wake up in the middle of the night and just sit in the den without lights, a radio or television. She began hiding her jewelry in odd places such as the dishwasher. Erratic sleep made her irritable, and she was completely uninterested in sex. Control issues became a major factor for her; unless her family did things on a precise schedule, she would fly into a rage, disappear into her bedroom and not come out until everyone promised to behave according to her rules.

As things went from bad to worse, her husband sought help from a local psychiatric hospital. Judy was diagnosed as a low bipolar manic depressive. Normally, manic depressives go on energy binges in which they sleep very little as long as they are "high." As they swing to low, they become withdrawn, uncommunicative and often paranoid. Judy's "high" was most people's normal. Her low was suicidal. It was as though her inner time sped up to hyperactive, then slowed down, creating very long periods in which there was no hope of dawn's light.

One day, when her husband was shopping at the local farmer's market, Judy packed a small suitcase and went to the airport, where she purchased a one-way ticket to Florida. Once there, she checked into a hotel, changed into a bathing suit and went to the beach. She walked into the water, and kept on walking until the ocean became too deep. She began to swim out to sea. Finally, exhausted, she let out all of her breath so that she could drown. As she sank deeper into the water, she suddenly found herself fighting for air. The next thing she knew, she was on the shore far down the beach from her hotel. She found her way back to the room and called her husband. He told her to catch the next plane back home. Oddly, she did that. He met her plane and took her to the psychiatric hospital and checked her in.

Her doctors recommended electroconvulsive therapy, or ECT. Because drugs such as lithium, which helps thousands of manic depression cases, had no effect on Judy, her husband agreed to this therapy. This process, formerly known as shock treatments, passes an electric current through the brain. It has been successfully used in many cases by removing all memory of the time the victim was ill. In Judy's case, it also removed the memory of having moved to her new home. She remembered her family, but had to relearn her friends, streets, shopping areas, even the recipes she had collected during that time. Yet for five years, Judy has remained at her "high" level, which renders her quite functional as a productive person.

No one knows why ECT works. Apparently it rearranges the brain chemistry electrically. At the same time, it resets biological clocks. Instead of speeding up and slowing down, the clocks get their phases reset and the depression lifts, often dramatically.

The rhythms of depression mock the rhythms of ordinary life. A depressed person's inner time goes by frighteningly slowly or quickly, making the victim feel at odds with the pace of everyday life. Hormonal shifts and temperature rhythms are unstable as well, shifting from day to day and causing apparent "better" days and "worse" days.

Ten million people suffer from depression, a condition that is looking more and more like out-of-phase biological clocks to some researchers. When chronobiologists began researching the field of depression, it did not take long for some fascinating questions and results to show up. Light cures, such as the phototherapy used in SAD, are being tried on some cases. Others appear to respond to moving sleep cycles backward about six hours. In one experiment, depression lifted for two weeks. In another trial, not sleeping at all for one whole night lifted the depression.

Sleep cycles coordinate with other hormonal and temperature cycles; adjusting one forces the others to reassemble the relationship. However, medical studies of the interrelationships of timing, dynamics and behavior are in their infancy. In experiments where skipping sleep lifted depression, it came back after the next sleep.

But why would adjusting a sleep cycle and forcing inner clocks to reset affect depression so dramatically? And how can science make this readjustment more permanent? Until just a few years ago, the timing of biological clocks was not thought to have an impact on mood affective disorders. But PMS and SAD have obvious connections to these biological rhythms. Scientists are now seriously examining the effects of biological clocks in this area.

The circadian clocks, attached to the circadian rhythms and therefore to OPS, may have interesting circuitry connections with depressions. Further research into chemical phase resetting of internal biological clocks will reveal amazing correlations between the activity of certain brain chemicals and circadian rhythms. Scientists have already noted that hormonal cycles are keyed to circadian rhythms. SAD and PMS are connected to the low point in the rhythms. Clinical depressions could also be in this mix. Do Optimum Gold times lift the moods of manic lows? Are there more suicides during Fair Reds periods? Does talk therapy help more during

Excellent Green and Moderate Blue times? Does the agitation of a manic high get more pronounced during Optimum Gold? Could scientists predict the curves in depression ahead of time by consulting OPS? We are on the edge of the frontier with these questions, and it may not be long before we can begin to settle the new land.

Stress

Ever since the cutting-edge research conducted by the renowned Canadian doctor Han Selye, stress has been the subject of much ado about something.

On the one hand, stress saves our lives. In emergencies, it pumps adrenalin to help us run faster, climb higher and get out of the way of a speeding truck. On the other hand, if we don't relax, we might as well let the truck hit us. Continued stress buildup gets the blame from many experts for ailments such as ulcers, heart disease, strokes, some cancers and a wealth of other conditions.

Chronobiologists did experiments on monkeys, subjecting them to continuous loud noises and uncomfortable heat over a long period of time. Very quickly, the monkey's inner clocks began speeding up. By the end of the experiments with humans, the results indicated that under stress, the monkeys and humans began operating on a 26- or 27-hour day rather than a regular circadian day or a 24-hour day.

Stress causes inner clocks to desynchronize, or fall out of time. The temperature cycle sings a different tune from the sleep cycle, making people awaken in the middle of the night, eat irregular meals and become more anxious. Sound like familiar behavior? If it does, you probably also know that there are a lot of stress-busting programs about, and lots of advice from experts on how to cure it.

It may be that resynchronization can be more easily achieved by following the OPS calendar. In part because it is a time-prioritizing system as well as a connection to the circadian clocks, OPS can help you become more in control and better able to respond to stressful situations. How? It allows you to consider how important each activity is in relation to its time segment. Putting things in perspective often relieves stress, and corresponding activity to biological time keeps those inner clocks ticking in perfect balance.

Sleep Disorders

A recent landmark book on biological clocks, *Inner Time* by Carol Orlock (Carol Publishing Group, New York, 1993), contains the most extensive coverage of the subject to date. She discusses the possibility of two "master clocks." One, the SCN that we have discussed earlier, appears to respond to light cues and regulates sleep, some hormones and reproductive cycles. This clock seems designed to allow phase resets by the owner. For example, the circadian "day" of 25 hours operates sleep cycles, which we adjust every day by resetting our sleep schedules to a 24-hour solar/lunar day.

Orlock mentions that the location of the other master clock seems uncertain, and that it seems to regulate internal temperature, which is critical to how alert one is and what mood one is in. REM (rapid eye movement) sleep is influenced by this "mysterious" clock, as well as some chemical and hormonal balances.

We believe the temperature clock is controlled by the circadian rhythms, the other "master clock." The two must coordinate schedules, and the one regulating temperature appears to be very resistant to change. For most of us, this is balanced by the precarious pendulums of our inner clocks. However, in some people, the daily temperature rhythms rise and fall on schedules other than the usual rise in the late afternoon and fall during the wee hours of the morning. These people often become victims of sleep disorders. Their sleep schedules become erratic, or simply drift. These people are wide awake all night, or sleep in fitful stretches. Most of the time, midday feels like 3 a.m. to them.

Doctors are beginning to treat sleep disorder victims with phototherapies as well as drugs. One study conducted by a blind postgraduate student in biostatistics on his own sleep/wake/activity cycles pegged him squarely on the longer circadian day. Once or twice a month, his "day" would coordinate with the rest of the waking world. His schedule was perfectly logical on circadian time, but because he needed to live in a 24-hour world, he began a low-glucose diet and tried light therapy. He was fine as long as he continued treatment, and his temperature began to rise and fall with the rest of us.

With some sleep disorders, resetting the internal temperature cycle may not be possible—or even desirable. Some studies document people who do their best work at night. These "owls" prefer that time, and many have adjusted well to night work and play. Their inner temperature cycles vary nearly two degrees—a whole degree more than daytime "larks"—and they spike at 3:00 *a.m.* rather than 3:00 p.m. or 4:00 p.m.

These people can be as productive as the rest of us, but are frequently forced to the margins of society simply because their inner clocks don't tick like the larks who fly in daylight. But there may be many more owls than previously thought. Note the popularity of wee-hour television shows and other all-night channels. Computer networkers are frequently found flying in their CompuServe cockpits overnight. Near Atlanta, Debbie Jordan of Cumming, GA produces the "Night Owl's Newsletter," a 16-page quarterly devoted to information helpful to people of the night. A Midnight Basketball League plays in 30 cities, an effort launched by executives of major corporations in an effort to curb nighttime violence in inner cities.

In fact, in his book *Night as Frontier: Colonizing the World After Dark* (Free Press, 1987), sociologist Murray Melbin likens the night owls to pioneers settling a new world, a world that has the lights on 25 hours per circadian day. This hypothetical world, perhaps filled with eccentrics in the larks' eyes, is not much different from our world when all is said and done. Melbin hopes that eventually the tolerance levels for different worlds will rise, and acceptance will be the order of the day (and night). Also on the rise will be the acceptance of the natural rhythms of our biological clocks.

People will be productive according to their body's time, whether 3:00 a.m. or 3:00 p.m.

The circadian rhythms and OPS seem quite important to productivity cycles and converting sleep disorders into ordered sleep. Optimum Gold times circulate throughout the night along with the other circadian segments. Night owls respond with high productivity during Optimum Gold and Excellent Green times at night, just as daytime larks produce heavily during Gold and Green times occurring during the day. OPS has exactly the same value to each type.

For those with insomnia, therapists can use OPS in their calculations to readjust sleep and temperature cycles. It may be much more difficult to make sleep cycles gear up to 90 minutes during the intensity of Optimum Gold times, and much easier during Fair Red or Moderate Blue. For those who seem to pop up wide awake in the middle of the night, OPS can play a part in predicting when those times might occur, and plans can be made to work with the circadian rhythms. For example, Optimum Gold times could be responsible for those pop-up times. It may be that some "disorders" are not disorders at all—the person with the problem could simply be responding to the intensity of their circadian rhythms.

When sleep-time melatonin hormone pills are developed, timing the dose to Fair Red periods may achieve better results. If wide-awake serotonin is needed, dosing it at an Optimum Gold could ensure success. Recognizing the need to add OPS to the mix of diagnostics and treatments could change the success rate in dealing with sleep disorders. Perhaps the future will bring a good night's (or a good day's) sleep to everyone.

Eating Disorders

Food can kill.

For people whose lives are not centered by food, this may seem improbable. But try telling that to the families of anorexics who have died. Anorexics genuinely believe being too thin is impossible. They starve themselves to death in order to be thin enough. Listen to the families of heart attack victims who never paid attention to the diet/exercise speeches of their doctors. Or to the friends of the bulimic whose esophagus was eaten away by years of bingeing and purging.

Tell it to Emerson McGhee, cross-addicted to food and alcohol just like his father was. His rationalization for weighing 330 pounds was that he knew alcoholics were always thin people. So he ate, became fat, and thought he couldn't be considered an alcoholic. He truly believed his logic.

Tell it to Diana, Princess of Wales. The difficulties of her fishbowl life were intensified by her struggles with bulimia, a disorder characterized by eating vast amounts of food and then throwing it all up afterwards.

We saw in chapter 4 that more people eat in Optimum Gold times than any other. In our restaurant study, nearly 22 more people per hour ordered a meal during Optimum Gold times than during Fair Red. The circadian rhythms obviously have an effect on when people eat, but what is their relationship to eating disorders, and how can OPS help?

People with eating disorders may be responding to the circadian rhythms in more ways than we now know. The intensity of each circadian time affects chemical and hormonal changes just as infradian and ultradian cycles do.

For example, studies have shown that bulimic women binge and purge more in the five days preceding their menstrual periods. The infradian clock regulating the menses evidently heightens their symptomatic behavior. Bulimics also binge more during autumn and winter, when the circadian rhythms are the least intense of the entire year. Optimum Gold periods in fall and winter cannot match the surges of spring and summer. Some chemical imbalance produced by hormonal and circadian shifts may contribute to the behavior of bulimics during these months. Would an Optimum Gold time during winter just before menses produce an uncontrollable need to binge more than any other time?

Anorexia victims, on the other hand, are depressed and unwilling to eat in the spring. This is also the time when it is easier to shed unwanted pounds. An ice cream sundae consumed in December lands on the hips.

One eaten in March gets burned up much more easily, apparently because of the increasing daylight. The more daylight there is, the more calories we burn, even when sitting still. All those people who go on diets on January first would have an easier time if they waited until the Ides of March! Of course, a true anorexic would not eat an ice cream sundae at any time. If she did, however, it would most likely be in December. In spring, she probably won't eat, perhaps because her biological clocks are telling her that she can lose more weight even faster during those months. The clocks don't know she has a life-threatening eating disorder. They are just doing their jobs. So it remains for her doctors to try and get the anorexic to eat more in the spring. Could they take advantage of Optimum Gold times to do that? Should meals be planned to capitalize on OPS times?

And what of compulsive overeaters? Could OPS be used to plan for times when out-of-control behaviors are most likely to take place? This particular disorder responds especially well to 12-step programs such as Overeaters Anonymous, in which members share problems and call one another when the "urge" to eat hits. Are these urges linked to circadian rhythms? If these uncontrolled times could be predicted with as much certainty as OPS can give, would it not be easier to treat a person suffering from this disorder? Should studies be made monitoring the eating habits of healthy people and those with eating disorders, and comparing their biological cycles of hormones and behavior?

Compulsive overeating and a condition known as carbohydrate-craving obesity, or CCO, appeared at first to be alike. After some study, however, researchers noticed that victims of CCO appeared to overeat only in the late afternoon and evening, and the object of desire was carbohydrate, not sugars, proteins or fats. This rhythmic cycling and nutrient specificity was proven to have a connection with the hormone serotonin, which lessens the need for carbohydrate and makes us feel happy and calm. Victims of CCO feel terribly depressed in the afternoons, and the carbohydrate bingeing lifts the depression. The bingeing forces the serotonin to kick in and make the victims happy—but fat. It is estimated that as many as two-thirds of obese people have CCO. And since almost half of

America's adult population is overweight, that's a lot of people. There are drugs that mimic the effects of serotonin, and these can be given to help people with CCO stop going to their carbohydrate heavens, so to speak.

The study of CCO in relation to eating disorders may prove to be groundbreaking. Eating disorders are identified by behavior, not by chemical analysis of which hormones are out of whack or what biological clock is out of phase. Much has been made of the low self-esteem component of many eating disorders, and a great deal of effort is made on the part of doctors to treat that. If these afflictions, as well as others, could be shown to be the result of chemical imbalances present perhaps from birth, surely treatment for them would be easier. And as scientists learn more and more about the influences of those inner clocks and circadian rhythms on our behavioral biology, the possibilities of cures become closer and closer.

OPS and Elder Care

Edwin Barrett spends his days in a world without time. A victim of Alzheimer's disease, a senile dementia medically diagnosable only in autopsy, Edwin exhibits all the behavior patterns that researchers have been able to identify with this disease. He cannot recall his family, does not speak and is unable to comprehend any speech. Occasionally, he appears to "surface" and interacts with those around him on a limited basis.

Most of the rest of his nursing home floor is filled with patients in some stage of Alzheimer's, which runs the gamut of behaviors from apparently functional to comatose. Fortunately for the patients, the nursing home staff tries to keep them active and involved in daily activities. But it is a nursing home environment, and many of the people there are unable to comprehend television, read, communicate with their comrades or interact with anything at all.

The efforts of the nursing home staff are not always successful. They complain that sometimes their charges won't eat, while at other times, they can't be fed fast enough. Visitors often notice that the floor is wild and rowdy on some occasions, quiet and ordered on others.

The staff credits the full moon for rowdy times, new moons for quiet ones.

We credit the circadian rhythms. This elder population, more than any other except perhaps babies, responds most purely to the circadian clocks. Because they live in a land without cognizance of external time structures, these patients are connected only to biological times. The time segments circulating through the circadian day uplift and subdue them just as they do ordinary people, but without the artificial time constraints of modern life.

We have observed that the times in which the staff cannot get the patients to eat correspond to Fair Red times in OPS. In Optimum Gold, they can't eat enough. Patients move from very mellow in Moderate Blue through alert and calm in Excellent Green. For some patients, Optimum Gold can bring those wonderful "surfacing" times, or it may produce severe agitation, depending on the chemical mix in the individual's makeup.

Were nursing home staffs able to work with the circadian clocks, following OPS to care for their patients, they would undoubtedly notice profound changes in the way patients go through their days. Feeding them in OPS times might keep their weight up, a constant problem in the elderly population. Recognizing the challenges Optimum Gold times can bring, extra staff can be added. Planning for middle-of-the-night Optimum Gold insomniacs could be made easier, and so could allowing for Excellent Green or Optimum Gold bedtimes. We understand that scheduling in nursing homes is difficult, but we would also like to make a plea for the patients. Allowing enough flexibility in the staffing schedules to put OPS into effect can enhance the lives of those who must live in institutions, and certainly make those who work in these environments happier with the results of their efforts.

SEVEN

PERSONAL BEST

XII
XI
I
X
II
IX

The OPS Personal Profile: It's You!

Initially, OPS was developed as an overall time management strategy that everyone could use in the same way. But when a clinical psychologist suggested that we study more personal applications of OPS, we decided to explore the possibilities. We discovered that knowing your personality characteristics and how you respond to the work environment—to co-workers and bosses and to stress situations—could make OPS work even better.

This chapter delves into the interplay between OPS and individual personality styles. With this segment of the OPS program, you can see how to match your personal best times with OPS times. First we'll look at three professionals during their work day, showing how each uses the OPS general program. Then we'll show you how each of these three people enhanced their productivity to even greater heights with help from our OPS Executive Performance Package (see page 152).

A Senior Real Estate Investment Analyst

Ken Weinberg's primary responsibility is analyzing potential real estate acquisitions for a large American insurance company's institutional clients. In his mid-twenties and single, Ken is very focused on his career, and has a laid-back, intellectual style. His typical work day begins between 8 a.m. and 9 a.m. and is broken down into the following duties:

* Review sales packages from various real estate brokers to determine whether properties meet investment criteria.

* Research the market and write up a deal summary with an initial pricing of the property.

* Talk with his boss to see if he might be interested in an acquisition.

* Make an in-depth analysis of the property value, tenants, competing properties and market demographics.

* Draw up a letter of interest for the seller and work with company attorneys in executing a contract.

* Phone various real estate brokers, internal portfolio managers and acquisitions consultants.

* Read newspapers, appropriate trade journals and business articles.

Once a month, Ken travels to properties in nearby states which are close to a deal or have a contract. He does not have to cross time zones, but does have to catch a plane at 7 a.m., and can expect to spend two days on the road. His travel workday includes:

* Driving around the market to see how the property his company is considering acquiring compares to the competition in such areas as location, accessibility, construction quality and tenant mix.

* Meeting with the property manager to discuss operational issues.

* Interviewing tenants.

* Meeting with structural and environmental consultants.

* Determining where the nice restaurants are for dinner.

Ken is able to schedule his workday pretty much to suit himself, most of the time arranging meetings according to his timetable. Unexpected interruptions in the form of telephone calls punctuate his day. He considers himself an "after 9:00 a.m. morning person", and likes to do his closely reasoned analytical work then, saving phone calls and meetings until after lunch. OPS time doesn't want to change his good habits, but would rearrange this system to go with the circadian rhythms pulsing through his day. Choosing a day at random, we picked a Tuesday in early spring to program for Ken. Each of his normal activities has been grouped in an OPS time best suited to it. As it happens, most of this day fits Ken's "morning person" attitude.

Ken's Typical Office Day Arranged to Optimize OPS

7:00 a.m. Moderate Blue	Wake up, eat breakfast and drive to office.
8:00 a.m. to 8:30 a.m. Moderate Blue\ 8:30 a.m. to 9:00 a.m. Fair Red	Arrive at office and read newspaper articles concerning properties.

9:00 a.m. Fair Red	Write letters of interest and deal summaries.
10:00 a.m. to 11:30 a.m. Fair Red	Review sales packages and work on in-depth analyses.
11:30 a.m. Optimum Gold	Talk to boss about possible acquisitions.
12:00 noon to 1:30 p.m. Optimum Gold	Lunch with real estate broker.
1:30 p.m. Optimum Gold	Phone brokers and consultants.
2:00 p.m. Optimum Gold	Review possibilities with boss.
3:00 p.m. to 4:30 p.m. Fair Red	Meet with attorney to work out contract negotiations.
4:30 p.m. Fair Red	Draft new letters of interest.
5:00 p.m. Fair Red	Prepare next day's agenda.
6:00 p.m. Moderate Blue	Leave the office. Work out at gym.
7:00 p.m. Moderate Blue	Prepare dinner at home.
8:00 p.m. Moderate Blue	Eat dinner.

Note that the afternoon contains a large Optimum Gold segment. For Ken, this is the best time for other people to listen to his analysis, as well as the best time for Ken to convince others of the merits or defects of a particular property. He spends the day's Fair Red times in his office retreat because this period favors objective analysis. Between 5:30 p.m. and 6:30 p.m., Ken drives to his gym in the rush hour, finding heavy but well-behaved traffic because the circadian rhythms are at their least intense.

On his travel days, we suggested to Ken an arrangement that would keep his "travel nerves" to a minimum. Since he has to arise at 5:00 a.m., when his body clocks are presiding over systems at their lowest ebb, Ken should adjust his agenda the previous evening to accommodate his travel plans. Then he will go to sleep the night before his 7:00 a.m. flight on a schedule that takes into consideration the 90-minute sleep cycles documented by sleep experts. In short, if he sleeps for seven and one-half hours or six hours, his sleep cycle will adjust more easily because his body's internal clocks cycle every one and a half hours. Ken should go to sleep at either 9:30 p.m. or 11:00 p.m. in order to get up easily at 5:00 a.m. If his alarm is set to wake him in an Optimum Gold time, getting up will be easier still; in a Fair Red period, more difficult. A trick he found helpful is to attach a timer to a bedroom light which he can set to go on at 5:00 a.m. Light, even through closed eyes, will help to reset his internal biological clocks.

If Ken traveled on the same day shown in his sample calendar on page 109, he would struggle awake during a 5:00 a.m. Fair Red time. Traveling in a Moderate Blue period is better than Excellent Green or Optimum Gold, but Ken was lucky to arrive at his destination at the beginning of a Fair Red time, which was perfect for extensive driving in the market area. During the Optimum Gold afternoon, he met with property managers and various consultants, interviewed tenants and finished his "research" on good restaurants. Dinner at 8:00 p.m., with one or more of the people he came to see, fit perfectly in that evening's Moderate Blue time. It was a very laid-back affair with no high-pressure sales tactics. Since Ken remained in the same time zone, his nighttime rest followed his regular schedule.

Ken used his OPS Executive Performance Package (see page 152) to optimize his travel time. In it, OPStravel Tips help travelers make the best use of the circadian calendars. Experts recommend several approaches for traveling between time zones. Ken used one or a combination of several for best results. Some of the tips include the following:

* If you are going to a location no more than two times zones away for over two days, adopt local time immediately. Otherwise, stay on your own time. If you must schedule important meetings, use the OPS calendar to set them in local OPStime. Your business prospects will improve, even if your own body clock is in another zone. If you must pitch new business or argue a case, do it in the Optimum Gold or Excellent Green time of your audience, even though your body clock remains in Fair Red or Moderate Blue. You will have to prepare twice as well, and motivate yourself harder, but you still have the edge—you're operating by OPS.

* Before you go, adjust as well as you can to the destination's time zone. Moving your meal and sleep schedule backward or forward 10 minutes every other day can acclimate you quite quickly.

* Avoid alcohol and overeating before flying. Liquor upsets temperature and hormone cycles, and a full stomach aggravates digestive problems. Instead, mineral water, a light meal and some exercise will prepare the body better.

* In flight, drink fruit juices and water. No alcohol.

* Break up long flights in one direction by layovers of at least a day. Business travelers who must visit several cities during the course of a week can plan cross-country schedules this way and avoid a constant feeling of desynchronization.

* Travel in your time zone during a Fair Red segment. Plan to arrive at your destination in an OPS time suited to your agenda and priorities.

* If flying west to east, take a morning walk to get used to light earlier than your body clock expects it. When traveling east to west, take walks to acclimate yourself to a later sunset.

A Second-Shift Quality Control Inspector

It was not until our present century that civilization found it necessary to work around the clock. Even in the Neanderthal period, guard duty was considered dangerous punishment, a tradition that has continued into modern times. Until the invention of the electric light bulb, only professions such as soldiering and medicine undertook overnight work. Electricity, combined with a burgeoning population that bought more things and needed jobs to finance them, made shift work a commonplace occurrence.

However, until very recently, the scheduling of shift work did not acknowledge our biological clocks. Until this decade, our inner clocks were something to overcome rather than work with, but now scientists are looking carefully at the biological rhythms that make us tick. Can they really be readjusted to produce optimum quality goods when our bodies are yearning for sleep? Can OPS help?

The answers to those questions are "sort of" and "yes." Because we as a society have not yet reached the point where chemical intervention—such as a melatonin pill to make us sleepy—is acceptable for resetting inner clocks, we must rely on such tricks as light therapies (see chapter 6). OPS can help because behavioral patterns are influenced by circadian rhythms. Our next example is a case in point.

Todd Hastings inspects the welded parts of automobile bodies in the swing shift, between 3:00 p.m. and 11:00 p.m. This is not the "graveyard" shift that everyone hopes their car was not assembled in, but it is one that has milder problems of the same kind—worker (and managerial) inattention, easily distracted workers, half-asleep management and a general sense of working overtime all the time. Todd's job includes looking for bad welds, making sure that the correct number of parts is produced on his shift and reaching his incentive goals by having the fewest mistakes.

He has noticed that there are good and bad shifts. Some evenings things go like clockwork, others are racked with problems and inefficiency. With OPS, he has learned to track the time segments and predict periods when people are mistake-prone. Although he has no control over the schedule for the assembly line itself, Todd can use OPS to improve his production quota.

Todd's day has an established pattern no matter what the circadian rhythms and OPS are doing. Because it takes him several hours to wind down from his job, he seldom gets to sleep before 1:30 a.m. His wife knows to keep the bedroom blinds down and the house quiet until about 9:00 a.m. to prevent the light from resetting Todd's internal clocks. If light hits Todd's eyes at 7:00 a.m., his automatic timing mechanism rephases and he loses sleep. Ordinarily, he rises at 9:00 a.m. and by 11:00 a.m. is taking a business class at a local university. When Todd arrives for work, his individual body clocks are on full-alert—and must remain so long after many of us have turned off the news and gone to sleep.

Todd's Workday, *Not* Arranged by OPS Time

3:00 p.m. Fair Red	Arrive at work, check personnel, and work on files.
4:00 p.m. to 5:00 p.m. Fair Red\ 6:00 p.m. Optimum Gold	Walk assembly line.
7:00 p.m.	Lunch.

Optimum Gold (Todd's "Noon")	
8:00 p.m. Optimum Gold	Attend conference with boss.
9:00 p.m. Optimum Gold	Monitor assembly line.
10:00 p.m. Optimum Gold	Do paperwork.
11:00 p.m. Optimum Gold	Leave work.

Todd's workday doesn't leave much room for independent scheduling, so the OPS advantage for him is his knowledge of how people—including himself—respond to given situations during various time periods. On this particular day, there was a shift from an easygoing Fair Red period to an intense Optimum Gold at 6:00 p.m. This was a great time for a conference with his boss, especially since he wanted to suggest a few changes in standard procedures. Accidents on the line are usually up during Optimum Gold periods, too, so Todd was especially watchful.

By the way, by following OPS on a daily basis, Todd was able to achieve his goals quickly and was promoted to a higher management position recommended by his boss because of his accurate knowledge of when events are most likely going to occur.

A Singer/Songwriter

Jannett Sibley composes songs and sings for a living. Married, in her late twenties, she lives in a comfortable bungalow in a midtown neighborhood of a large city on the east coast. It is a short commute to the recording studio and to the places where she tries out her new material. About once a year, she travels extensively to promote a new album or to sing on a concert tour.

She sees herself as a night person—chronobiologists would call her an owl—because nothing in her body seems to function before noon. Her best times are the late evening and even into the wee morning hours. Scientists tell us that whether we are owls or day people, called larks, the quality is built into each of us genetically. Most people perform better in the morning or afternoon; extremes on either end are the people who function best at night. Jannett is one of those; her daily temperature cycle hits its peak in the late evening rather than in the afternoon as most people's do.

Into each professional day, she needs to fit band or orchestra rehearsals, voice lessons, creative time for composing, meetings with her agent or other members of the music community, performances and travel time. In her personal life, she must schedule time with her husband, who luckily plays flute with the local symphony orchestra and shares her owl tendencies.

Because Jannett's "day" really begins at noon, her OPS time can be adjusted to fit—the circadian rhythms move all the time, so all one has to do is catch the next song, so to speak. She is able to control her schedule more than most, except in one area: performances. She finds audiences on their feet for her in Optimum Gold times, but dead in their seats in Fair Red. How does she compensate for this?

Realizing that her audience may be least responsive in the late evening anyway because the melatonin supplied to their brains by their ultradian clocks is making them sleepy, and that performing in a Fair Red period is just going to make this worse, Jannett tries to schedule performances in more auspicious color times. The inherent nature of performance influences mood, so if a Fair Red time must be dealt with, she choreographs fast rhythm numbers and upbeat melodic lines in her sets. This is no time for melancholy love songs. And over at the symphony, program producers can look months ahead to schedule the evening's order; Dvorak's *largo* movement from his *New World Symphony* will surely put the audience asleep in a Fair Red time. Better to get people going with Carl Orff's Carmina Burana.

For rehearsals, voice lessons, and creative time for composing, Jannett chooses less intense circadian periods. Excellent Green times are great for meetings with her agent or other members of the music community. The Moderate Blue times can accommodate her composition demands. Her travel times need to be scheduled in Fair Red periods whenever possible, and sleep scheduled to adjust in advance to a different time zone. Since it is always easier to adjust to times zones going west, Jannett pays a lot of attention to readjusting to eastern time before returning home.

Since Jannett rarely rises before noon, we adjusted her schedule to run from noon to 3:00 a.m. the following morning.

For Jannett, this particular day has a Fair Red period when her performance begins. If she makes an effort to involve her audience with some powerhouse music, she can sweep them into whatever mood she chooses to create after 10 p.m. when the Optimum Gold segment starts. As for her audience, they will just feel increasingly interested in Jannett's music as the evening progresses.

Jannett's Workday Arranged by OPS Time

12:00 noon Excellent Green	Wake up and have breakfast.
1:00 p.m. to 2:30 p.m. Excellent Green	Meet with agent, producer.
3:00 p.m. Fair Red	Go over correspondence and write letters.
4:00 p.m. Moderate Blue	Voice lesson.
5:00 p.m. to 7:00 p.m. Moderate Blue	Work on new songs/composition.

7:00 p.m. Fair Red	Her "lunch."
8:00 p.m. Fair Red	Dress for performance.
9:00 p.m. Fair Red	Performance.
10:00 p.m. to 11:00 p.m. Optimum Gold	
12:00 p.m. to 3:00 a.m. Optimum Gold	Dinner and catch club acts.

Personality Style and OPS

The three people whose workday lives we have been examining have differing personality styles as well as careers. We wanted to find out how those styles could use OPS to enhance not only their productivity, but their relationships within the work environment. Using a well-known personality analysis workbook, we were able to help each person understand his and her own characteristics and how to match them to OPS time for the most favorable results.

Each of our examples were chosen because the position fits the person—and the inner biological clocks each possesses. We mentioned Jannett's "owl" personality; Ken seems to be a "lark," and Todd appears able to fly as either bird. Jannett's lifestyle works because her inner clocks are set that way. Ken would be miserable with her schedule.

Most people gravitate toward work that ticks to their inner clocks. We have looked further into our examples to see how each individual could use OPS to even further advantage.

We mentioned that Ken has a laid-back, intellectual style. His office manager is a prima donna emotional type who flutters from office to office clucking over the condition of desks. She seems to have difficulty connecting to Ken, who is shy to the point of being withdrawn. How can OPS help Ken here?

With the aid of our OPS Executive Performance Package, Ken was able to figure out how his mild, reserved and soft-spoken style could be used to communicate with his manager, despite her more talkative, outspoken ways. He realized that he seemed curt and too focused on facts and figures for her. Instead, he needed to ask how she feels about things and give her the impression that he would like to be friendly. By watching how his manager responded to the four OPS time segments, Ken also reasoned that she was most calm during Fair Red periods. Ken decided to seek her out during those times to take care of any business they might have. Their relationship improved considerably after this change.

The value of our analysis brought objectivity to what had been simply an emotional conflict for Ken and the office manager. By understanding her agenda, and in what OPS time she would be most receptive to him, Ken was able to change the situation favorably.

Todd Hastings, in his early thirties, married and earning a bachelor's degree in business administration, knows that his swing-shift job is a stepping stone to better days. To that end, he is very conscientious about his position, very much a team player and a highly disciplined worker. Not much escapes his notice, and if something does, he will be as hard on himself as on the worker who caused the incident.

For some time, Todd has been at odds with a welder who appears to be a highly competitive risk-taker. The worker even bets others he can finish more welds than anybody else in a given time period. This person does excellent work, but because he is constantly competing with himself—not to mention everybody else—he makes mistakes.

With our help, Todd understood that this man's independent style and daring ways interfered with Todd's need for an ordered, detail-oriented and predictable workday. By monitoring the OPS times, he knew that the worker did more work, but also made his biggest mistakes, in Optimum Gold times. During those times the man seemed very aggressive and worked fastest. Todd sought him out during a Moderate Blue time to praise his work habits and motivation. Next, he discussed how well the worker performed at certain times and the problems that repeatedly occurred during Optimum Gold times. He gave the worker a list of times during the next two weeks in which caution needed to precede speed. Given this approach, it did not take long for the worker to realize that Todd wanted to work with, rather than against him, and Todd came to recognize the man's leadership abilities in increasing the line's productivity.

Jannett's OPS Executive Performance Package revealed an intensely creative style. Strong-willed, independent and goal-oriented, she must temper her style to charm and entertain her audience. Her music uses a strong classical base in a highly evocative, bluesy, contemporary way. For this, she also needs to exhibit a soft femininity. Yet during contract negotiations, she requires a strong, no-nonsense approach. From working with the Personal Plan, Jannett has discovered that all these elements are present in her personality and that she can manage them by optimizing her OPS time. She likes to finalize contract negotiations during Optimum Gold Times when she is at her most persuasive and convincing. More objective meetings yield good results in Excellent Green times, and she reserves her Moderate Blue times for composition. These times have proven so productive for her, in fact, that she has become quite adamant about protecting her "creative" time.

OPS is an interactive program. Because of its groundbreaking technology, the work we have set out to do has really just begun. We have made great inroads into optimum performance technology, and the people who have been working with it for some time now are very connected to it. Because of this technology's great impact on society at large, we also want your input into the system. If you have been working with the General Schedule, and find yourself curious about ways to improve your productivity even more, we are here to help you on a personal basis. Write us at the following address:

Optimum Performance Technologies
Post Office Box 2164
Roswell, Georgia 30075
404/998-8107

We'll send you the details of our OPS Executive Performance Package, which includes an extensive personality profile and workbook. Use them to match your personality style with OPStime, and explore a wide range of support materials to broaden your personal application. If you wish, we can put you on our list of Charter Subscribers. These individuals will receive a one-year OPS Performance Package containing a questionnaire, which is our Style Analysis Instrument, a color schedule of the next two months of OPStime, a cassette tape welcoming subscribers to the program, a user-friendly brochure with inside tips on OPS and return mailers. When you return the initial questionnaire, we'll send you a 14-page report on your individual style that includes a workbook on how to use what you've learned, and a schedule of two additional OPS months. Every twelve weeks, you send us a mailer, and we'll respond with ways to make your OPS Executive Performance Package work to its highest degree of effectiveness.

During the year, we'll also keep in touch with personal letters and our newsletter, in which you can read about people just like yourself and how they have used the program to be more successful. You could even be reading about yourself!

When you "graduate" at the end of your year, you won't need a diploma, but you will need the next year's OPS schedule, so we'll give you a twenty percent discount coupon for OPS products. Nobody else will get this discount. It's our way of saying thank you to our Charter Members.

Of course, everything you need to begin using OPS immediately is outlined in this book. It is simply that we couldn't possibly include every OPS application, and we know from experience that working personally with people

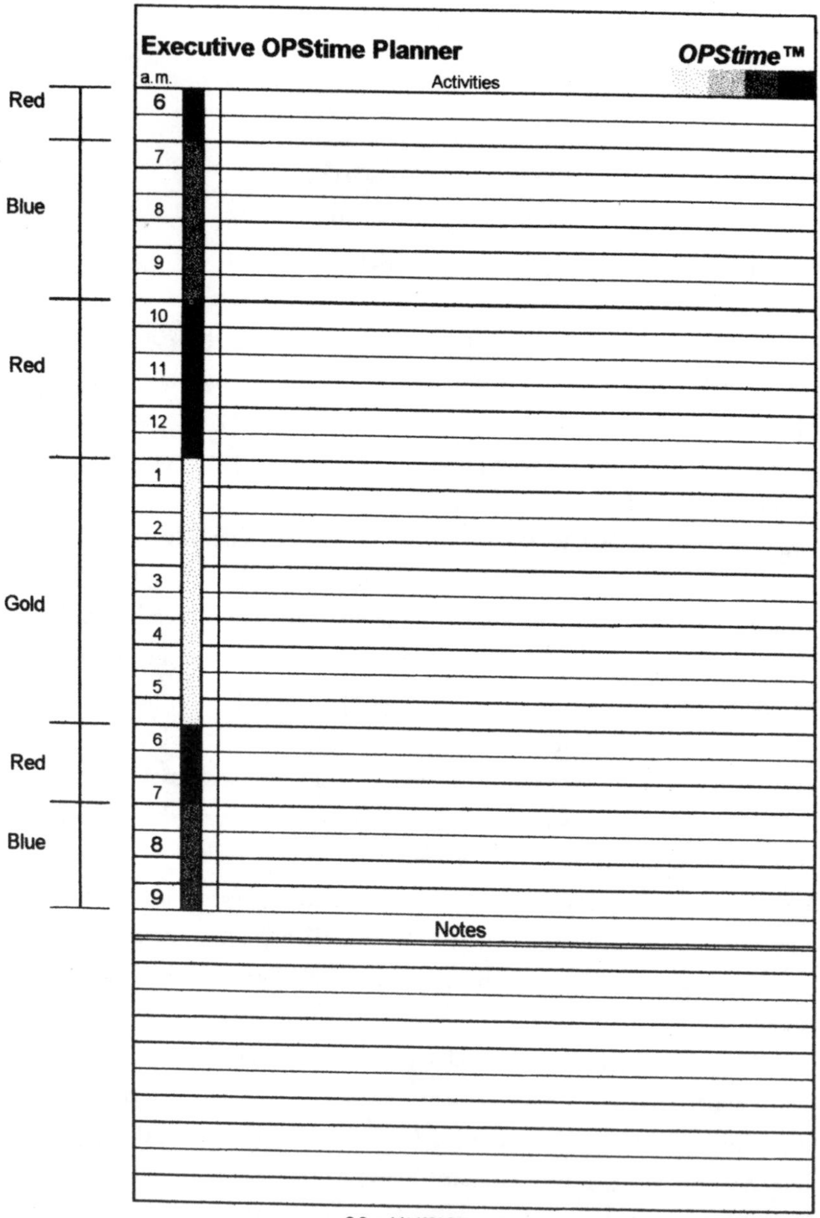
Executive OPStime Planner
OPStime™
a.m.
Activities
Red
Blue
Red
Gold
Red
Blue
6
7
8
9
10
11
12
1
2
3
4
5
6
7
8
9
Notes

© Copyright 1994 Optimum Performance Technologies

This is a sample of the Executive OPStime Planner. The Executive OPStime Planner includes the following: full color calendar, executive personality profiler, introductory cassette, OPS tips pamphlet, quarterly newsletter, and OPStech phone support.

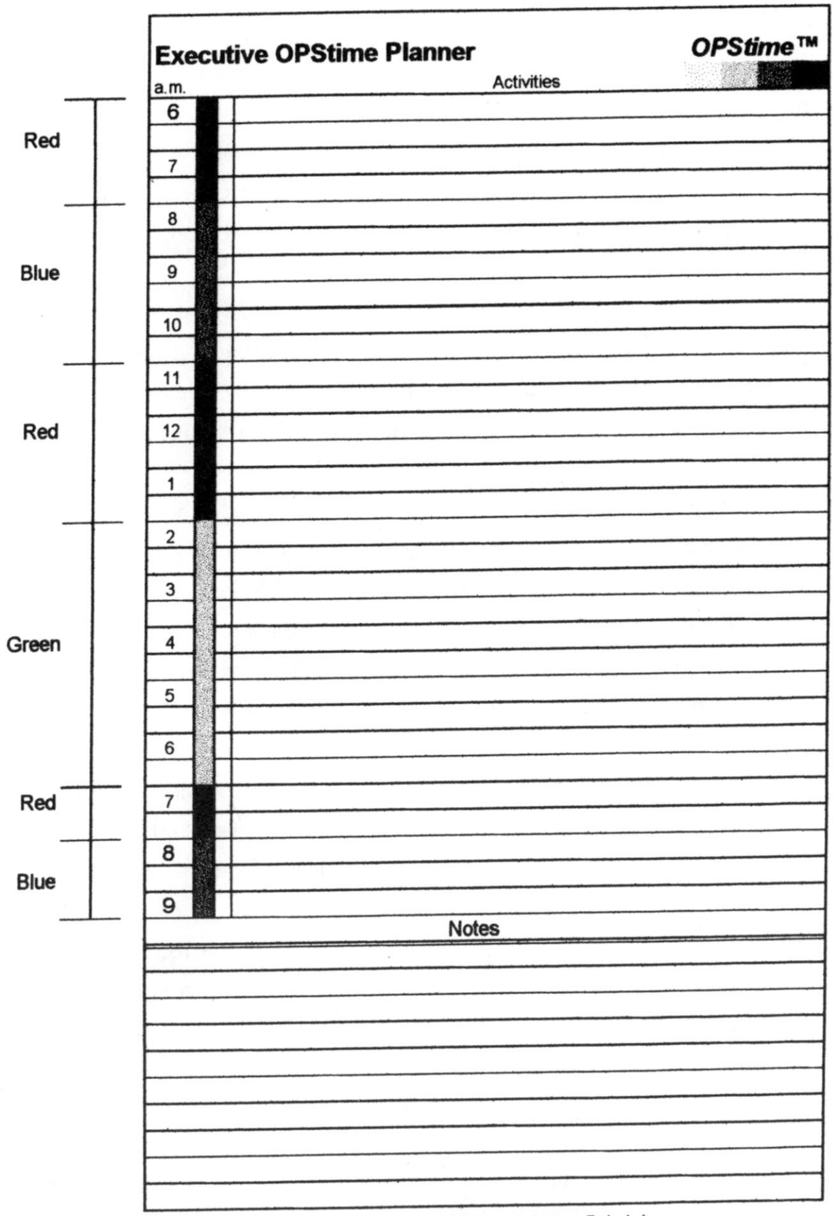
Executive OPStime Planner
OPStime™
a.m.
Activities
6
7
8
9
10
11
12
1
2
3
4
5
6
7
8
9
Red
Blue
Red
Green
Red
Blue
Notes

© Copyright 1994 Optimum Performance Technologies

This is a sample of the Executive OPStime Planner. The Executive OPStime Planner includes the following: full color calendar, executive personality profile, introductory cassette, OPS tips pamphlet, quarterly newsletter, and OPStech phone support.

garners the greatest rewards from the program. But you are certainly welcome to use what is in this book on your own. We'd like to hear from you, so please write to let us know how you're coming along.

No matter what field you are in, the benefits of structuring your days on OPStime are great. Here are some examples of how the program works in a variety of areas:

* Sales Managers: Hiring the right people and motivating them to perform at peak levels takes more than know-how. It takes know-*when*, and OPS has a ready-made, simple schedule to take the guesswork out of timing.

* Telemarketing: Everybody in the industry knows the "golden hours" between 5:00 p.m. and 8:00 p.m. are the times when they can reach the most people. Closing sales ratios can go up dramatically with OPS: Potential customers in varying time zones can be contacted in *their* Optimum Gold, Excellent Green or Moderate Blue times. Fair Red times can be bypassed in those zones and concentration focused on others where timing is better.

* Executive Secretary: The person who makes the boss's schedule has a distinct advantage in using OPStime. When the boss has a critical deal in the making, his secretary needs to know when to clear his/her appointments calendar.

* Consultants: Successful consultants in any field have a sixth sense for problem areas and obstacles to overcome. With their nose for nuisance systems, they can use OPS as part of their own sensitivity training as well as know when to make reports and give suggestions for change. Integrating people, processes, strategies and technologies can be timed better with OPS.

* Architects: Wouldn't you like to know when a client is going to be receptive to ideas? Instead of trusting luck, OPS determines specific times for client meetings when optimum results can occur. OPS can also clue you in to the best times for using your creative energies and for working out engineering details.

* Attorneys: Criminal lawyers have little control over when trials are scheduled. Given the luck of the draw, OPS can help attorneys over-come the lethargic juries of Fair Red Times, make their most impassioned pleas during Optimum Gold, and present their most complicated logic in Excellent Green. If it's the wrong time, OPS is a tool for making it right.

* Development Directors: With all the world competing for the same dollar, how does one development director get an edge over another? Networking helps, and so does being friendly with every CEO's Executive Assistant, but *knowing* when Mr. CEO is likely to be most responsive to your requests for support gives you an advantage that is practically unfair.

* Construction Foremen: How can the times when workers are most likely to hammer thumbs, drop bricks and make the walls off plumb be predicted? OPS Optimum Gold times see more accidents than any other. It seems that the best time for sales turns out to be the worst time for constructin buildings . . . cars . . . widgets. . . .

* Customer Service Representatives: How many times have you answered the telephone to find an irate customer? As this customer's only human link to the services your company offers, you're well aware of your friendly, problem-solving role. How can you tell when customers will be at their most irate, the time when you must be truly diplomatic? Consult OPS. Optimum Gold times will provide you with the times you're likely to encounter the most annoyed people. Least intense times, the lowest being Fair Red, could give you a breather from the dragons. If you knew ahead of time to brace yourself and adjust your style for difficult times, wouldn't your job performance reviews improve?

* Truck Drivers: We can't say, "just leave the driving to OPS," but we can tell you when the roads will likely be their worst and when you can relax and just go along for the ride. Independent of weather, the circadian rhythms OPS is based on glide through each day bringing different patterns to each one.

Drivers attuned to the changes can adjust their schedules across a city or across the country to balance their day for easier—and safer—driving.

EIGHT

A MAGIC CARPET RIDE

The Future Runs by the OPS

Though OPS staffers are not given to flights of fancy as a general rule, they wanted to add a chapter on applications of untested theories, but ones that are logical extensions of current research. In the previous chapters, we have relied on empirical and anecdotal evidence to guide us in how to use OPStime to enhance productivity and prioritize goals. Here, theory and imagination can take wing, providing new insights, fresh approaches and some plain fun.

Back into Time

One staffer, a history buff, wanted to know the influence of circadian rhythms on historical events. What if the Greeks tried to sell the ploy of the Trojan Horse in a Fair Red time, when the Trojans weren't buying? Did Napoleon lose Waterloo because he didn't fight in an appropriate OPS time? Was the invasion of Normandy a success because the Allies were in the right place at the right OPS time? When do military leaders make decisions?

Should they know what OPStime it is before they make one? Since people are at their most impassioned during Optimum Gold and Excellent Green periods, should former president George Bush's decision to bomb Iraq in Operation Desert Storm have been made during one of these times? Should pilots actually fly their missions in Optimum Gold or at a less intense time when the enemy is not as alert?

What if an Optimum Gold time spurs an impulsive military decision that, reconsidered in a less intense time, would not have been made? Since we cracked the circadian code, we can go back and retrace our circadian steps to ascertain in which OPS times battles were won or lost, or which plans might have produced better results if the decision makers had used a more appropriate OPS time. For example, if negotiations for the release of the hostages in Iran had been made during an Optimum Gold time, would we have had an earlier release? And what if diplomatic efforts had taken OPStime into account during "shuttle diplomacy" missions? Surely the jet lag factor shot down many a talk; if our diplomats had been on OPS time, their goals might have been more easily accomplished.

The World According to OPS

Another member of our team is interested in the political effect of OPS. Are we more susceptible to the opinions of politicians in certain OPS times? Would American foreign policy be more successful if summit meetings were scheduled for Optimum Gold times? Have treaties been negotiated in OPS times in which their success or failure could have been changed? What if President Jimmy Carter just happened to have negotiated the Camp David Accords in Optimum Gold and Excellent Green periods?

Would taxpayers be more surly when news of higher taxes reached them in an Optimum Gold or Excellent Green time? Will Congress schedule votes to implement pay raises or unjustifiable tax increases in Fair Reds in the hopes that people won't be as attentive? Does Bill Clinton need to address Congress and the American people in a particular OPS time to be more effective? Could he sway Congress to act on his health plan in Excellent Green? What if the vote is scheduled in a Fair Red—should the Democrats try to get the vote scheduled for an Optimum Gold or Excellent Green time?

Because people are ready to listen and buy, and salespeople are at their peaks, the two most intense times in the circadian rhythms might be the best time for Clinton and his people to work on the legislative branch, both during debates and voting. We believe the same process could be implemented for NATO and United Nations meetings; the best time to sway an assembly would be during the Optimum Gold and Excellent Green segments.

Accidents

When we discussed Ken Weinberg's travel arrangements in chapter 7, we were able to make some accurate predictions because of the preliminary empirical studies we had made on accidents (see chart, page 130).

We found the safest times to travel were Fair Red, with Optimum Gold being the worst time. We attribute this to the intensity of the time segment. In Fair Red, people seem slower, are more amiable and drive defensively; in Optimum Gold, people behind the wheel become much more aggressive and drive offensively. Statistically, the absolute worst time to be on the road is during the wee hours of a Sunday morning. Not only are the last of the party-goers driving with too much alcohol and melatonin in their bloodstreams, but we would make an educated guess that adding an Optimum Gold to that time period would worsen the situation. A further study we conducted on the times traffic tickets were given confirmed our predictions about Optimum Gold speeders. An Optimum Gold time combined with a rainy-day rush hour would be a lousy time to be on the road.

What about rapes? How about homicides and suicides? Crimes of violence should show a distinct pattern even given the known influencing factors

Comparison of Percent of Day in Each OPS Time with Actual Number of Accidents

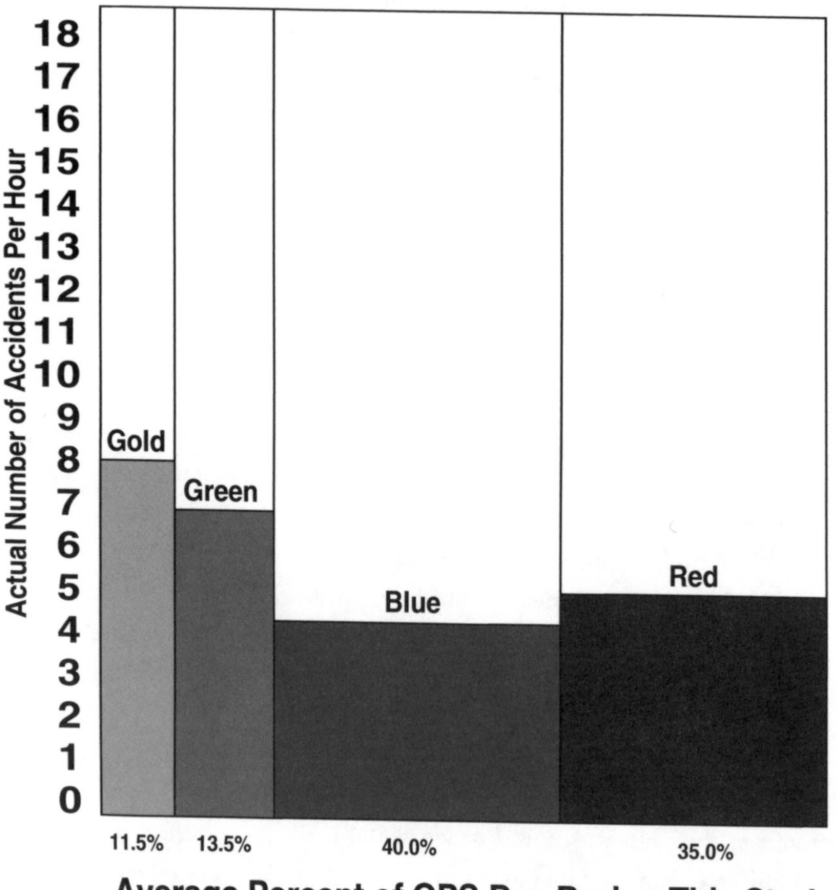
Actual Number of Accidents Per Hour
18
17
16
15
14
13
12
11
10
9
8
7
6
5
4
3
2
1
0
Gold
Green
Blue
Red
11.5%
13.5%
40.0%
35.0%
Average Percent of OPS Day During This Study

of Saturday nights, weather and season. Most criminal justice divisions in large cities already know crime waves rise during summer's heat. Adding OPStime to current knowledge could help administrations know when to add staff ahead of time, and help people in their precincts stay out of harm's way. What if High Crime Alerts could be posted for the next Saturday night's Optimum Gold time? Statistical studies comparing OPS times to 911 calls may show a preponderance of these crimes occurring in the most intense time segments of the circadian day. With respect to suicides, the staffs of hospitals, institutions and jails should be notified that potential suicides may act in Optimum Gold time segments.

The influence of the circadian rhythms, long acknowledged but never given enough credit, could truly be the answer to some of society's biggest problems.

A Spot for Sports

It's the bottom of the ninth inning. David Justice is at bat for the Atlanta Braves in their last-ditch attempt to wrest the World Series away from the Toronto Blue Jays. The pitch . . . the swing . . . a hit! It's over the fence! Braves win! Dizzy with delight, Atlanta parties the night away. . . .

Did OPS predict the win? You bet. Along the way, OPS staffers figured out a way to change the way bookmakers operate in Las Vegas. It's an intriguing *tour de force* use of OPS for fun and games. Imagine the football, basketball, baseball and hockey seasons rising and falling on the strength of OPS.

You can try predicting outcomes for yourself. You'll need an OPS calendar, a play schedule and one special piece of information: Bodies reset their internal biological clocks to different time zones at the rate of two hours per solar/lunar day. That means a Georgian in California's time zone will take one and a half days to phase in to the West Coast's three-hour time difference. You'll also need to know the length of time between arrival of the team and the game. Figuring out what body clock time each team is playing in can predict the win, especially with teams equal in skills and league standings.

With the Atlanta Braves as an example, we'll explore several outcomes of imaginary games. In the first, the Braves arrive a day before a game with the Los Angeles Dodgers. The game is scheduled to begin during a Fair Red time and end about an hour into Optimum Gold. Braves lose. Why? Because their internal clocks haven't adjusted to California's OPS time segments. The Dodgers take advantage of playing terrific ball as they swing into their Optimum Gold time—with the Braves lagging behind both internally and on the scoreboard.

In this case, OPS may be the secret to home field advantage. When everything else is just about equal, OPS hits the home runs.

In another case, the Braves arrive in Los Angeles just a few hours before the game. Without time to reset inner clocks, they play in their own Optimum Gold time against the Dodgers who are striking out in Fair Red. Braves win.

OPS can't make a bad team good, but the circadian rhythms can affect the scores of even the greatest teams. And what if both teams have games scheduled in Optimum Gold? That's when all the other statistical factors come into play. Your guess is as good as OPS then!

To win a more down-home field advantage, take a look at Little League. What if you could tell your son when he needed to play hardest to win and when the peak time for his team was going to be? If the game is scheduled in a Fair Red, for example, what's it going to take to overcome the inertia? If you are able to identify this time period, your son's team can take advantage of it by capitalizing on the other team's down-time response to the circadian rhythms.

In and Out of Time

If an airline advertised that it could get you there and back without your suffering the effects of jet lag, wouldn't you hop aboard? If your travel agent could guarantee vacations with almost no jet lag, wouldn't you be on his permanent client list?

Think how terrific it would be if you touched down at Orly airport bursting with energy and ready for Paris. Even the first night, you go to sleep at a reasonable time (perhaps for you, anyway—Parisians have never found time reasonable at all).

This happy occasion is yet to arrive, but research is getting closer to the day when adjusting to time changes will be no more difficult than putting on different clothes. The secret appears to be a combination of two things: melatonin and controlled phase resets of biological clocks. In chapter 6 we explored how melatonin levels rise in the bloodstream during the evening hours, making people ready for sleeping. In a study conducted on a group traveling from London to California, some people were given melatonin before and after the trip and some people were given placebo pills. The melatonin worked 100 percent of the time. Melatonin is already given to blind people whose reset mechanisms cannot operate on light cues, so regulatory agencies already accept its uses in human subjects. It may not be long before its uses in time-phase resets will become more widespread.

The problem with melatonin is *when* to take it. The hormone readjusts body-temperature cycles, so that the delicate biological clock mechanisms depending on temperature cycles theoretically fall into line when the temperature is reset. Taking a melatonin pill in London before a flight, which sets the traveler back in time eight hours before he reaches California, would have the net effect of creating an entire nighttime. If the plane left Heathrow at 8:00 a.m., arrival in California nine hours later (with a stopover for fuel) would put the travelers on the tarmac at 5:00 p.m., body time and 9:00 a.m. California time. With their eyes well-covered to prevent daylight from reaching the optic nerve and interfering with their melatonin therapy, the travelers have a good "night's" rest on the trip, and the jet lag suffered is minimal to none. If the traveler left Heathrow in an OPS Fair Red time, the melatonin would allow an even deeper restful state.

Without the melatonin or OPS, the net effect would be one of having stayed up an extra eight hours, or going to sleep at perhaps 2:00 p.m. and waking up again at 9:00 p.m. ready to sightsee. This fall out of time causes the dizziness, disorientation and partial amnesia of jet lag (desynchronization to a chronobiologist).

On the return trip, leaving Los Angeles at 8:00 a.m. after adjusting to California time means that body time at touchdown at Heathrow will be 6:00 p.m. Ready to party? Sorry—London's asleep at 2:00 a.m. (except for Soho). If the traveler has made sure that his arrival will be made in a Fair Red time according to his California-tuned inner clock, taking the melatonin upon touchdown can insure a good night's sleep, though don't expect to be at work at 8:00 a.m. London time. Give your body until noon.

Without the hormone and OPS, arrival back in London will be twice as horrible in terms of jet lag because it is always easier to travel west to east than the reverse. Researchers believe this is due to the fact that the 25-hour circadian day naturally slides biological clocks forward. Backing up from west to east means literally losing time. Daylight Savings Time illustrates this well: statistically, accidents for a week after the time change go up 10 percent. People call in sick for work. Absenteeism is up in schools for a week. And that's just a one-hour adjustment! For those who suffer jet lag the most—and some people just don't seem affected by it very much for reasons we don't yet understand—even Monday mornings bring on the blues. When these people travel, the desynchronization effects are major. When melatonin, along with its wide-awake sidekick serotonin, become available to "cure" jet lag, these out-of-phase folks will be the first in line.

OPS in My Job Description

When do you have the best chance of landing that job you wanted? You guessed it—Optimum Gold and Excellent Green. You may not be able to control when the potential employer reads your resume, but you can try to schedule the interviews according to OPStime.

And that raise . . . what if you decide to politic for it in a Fair Red? Sorry—try again in the upper intensity levels of OPStime. If you're going for a promotion, shouldn't you make sure your golden (Optimum Gold, that is) opportunities present themselves at the right OPS time?

Suppose you have to make a speech. If this is something you don't do all the time, public speaking can be quite intimidating. Check the OPS times on the date. You can be sure your audience is going to respond according to what circadian time it is. If not Optimum Gold, adjust your speech to accommodate the time. If it's in a Fair Red, at least you've identified part of the potential problem and can work to overcome it. If you can, schedule the speech or presentation at a better time.

If your profession involves the law, wouldn't it be great if you knew when the jury would listen to your final argument? You should know by now to go for the Gold. If you must present in Fair Red, you will at least be prepared to try and overcome the jury's lack of interest. Since court dates and trials are definitely scheduled without any consideration for OPS time, it's up to you to take advantage of the circadian rhythms. You could always try for a continuance. Polling juries might be best in Excellent Green; getting the best of the other side's star witness might be achieved in Fair Red because you know how to take advantage of the decreased intensity in the rhythms.

If you are thinking of retaining legal services, you may want to ask if your potential attorney is on OPStime.

Those of you who staff the various psychiatric professions know better than most how moods affect your patients. What if you could predict when Mrs. Jones is going to solve some of her long-standing problems? What if you knew ahead of time that Mr. Parsons gets so blue during Fair Red times that he's hard to talk to? Nurses often look out on a waiting room filled with cranky, irritable people. Do they know what OPS time it is? We'll bet Fair Red. If the people are patiently reading magazines and not fidgeting, we'll bet on Moderate Blue.

If you want to get ahead in your chosen profession, and have to go to graduate school to achieve your goals, is there a best time to take those GREs? Often you have an option of days to take it. Our recommendation is go for the Gold. And that goes for Bar Exams, Medcats, ACTs and SATs as well.

OPS . . . Your Life and Style

One of our OPS staffers proposed marriage in an Optimum Gold time. Now, who can say that was what swayed his beloved's decision? However, our staffer would never trust something as important as that to a less intense time segment. And it is true that people are more receptive during Optimum Gold! The answer was positive. Our lucky groom scheduled an August wedding in an Excellent Green time so the lucky lady would be less tearful because of the lesser intensity of that time.

Here at Optimum Performance Technology, we literally live life by the Optimum Performance Schedule. We check our schedule for social events and other important things. One staffer considers the best OPS time for artificial insemination; she figures her biological clocks will coordinate on the circadian rhythms. Another won't go out on a date during a Fair Red period. Still another checks the OPS calendar for the best romantic times (of course it's Optimum Gold, and these often can be found in the middle of the night). Our aforementioned groom made sure his honeymoon cruise contained plenty of Optimum Gold.

For events involving more than two people, we check the calendar to schedule parties and plan them for the more intense times. If attending a play or a concert, we'll buy tickets for the night we believe we'll see the best performances, which would be anything but Fair Red. Those of us who like to visit the health club go for the upper intensity levels, too. Exercise just seems to work more magic in those times. It doesn't have to be "no pain, no gain" when you work out in Optimum Gold or Excellent Green. The body seems to have a higher tolerance to pain in those time periods. One staffer likened the differences between running in various OPS times to the difference between running in combat boots and running in sneakers.

And when our vehicles break down, when do we schedule the work? You know. Why would we want mechanics fixing a car in Fair Red? We can only hope that our cars weren't manufactured originally in a Fair Red time on a Monday.

Have you ever sat down to have a heart-to-heart chat with someone you love and he or she behaved as if you didn't exist? Perhaps among the many factors involved, you didn't approach them in the right OPS time. Have you ever gone to counseling or therapy sessions and gotten nowhere? Once again, the wrong OPS time was probably the culprit. Take time to explore the various OPS times' effects on yourself and those around you.

We've lived with the schedule long enough that we're intimately connected to the circadian rhythms. They have become an integral part of our lives, just like eating and breathing. We see the influence of OPStime everywhere, even in the smallest incidents. Remember in the introduction when I spoke of being in the mall in what happened to be an Optimum Gold time (though I didn't know it then)? People were lined up at the cash registers. When you start looking around, connecting what you see to OPStime, amazing insights will begin to occur to you as naturally as the clock moves forward. Living your life on OPStime will help insure that you can perform at your peak all of the time instead of some of the time.

As Good as Gold

By now you have an inkling of some of the potential uses for OPS. By no means have all of them been discovered or explored. The only limit to the usage of OPStime is your own imagination. OPS can affect virtually every facet of your existence. There is a veritable treasure trove of OPS applications out there for you to unearth. If you have ever dreamed of being Marco Polo and discovering new worlds, you have your chance at last. As you explore the new world of OPS, drop us a note from time to time and let us know where your journeys take you and what you discover along the way. Perhaps in the next book you may be reading about your own explorations or those of someone you introduced to OPS.

Though the explorations in chronobiology are just beginning, and the results modest, the possibilities for applications are nearly limitless. At Optimum Performance Technologies, we live by the OPS calendar, and every day discover new applications of the system and ways it can provide more order to our lives. For many of us, OPS has given sense and reason to previously unexplainable behaviors. We have become more tolerant and more understanding of people's moods. But more than that, the stories we have gathered in the course of research and the people we have worked with have proven that OPS can make the difference. After all is said and done, they have shown us that OPS times are the best times of our lives!

The OPStime charts that I have provided in this book will allow you to apply the Optimum Performance Schedule to your daily life. By acting now, you will be at the forefront of this breaking technology—one that is sure to impact every phase of society in the coming years.

Just in Case

We hope you have an understanding of how OPS can improve your productivity and enhance your life. To help you along the first steps of discovering the dramatic difference OPS can make, we have included a general schedule of OPS times. The following pages cover a twelve month period—from June 1, 1994 through May 31, 1995. We want to make sure you have a full twelve months of usable OPS times so that you can take advantage of what OPS has to offer. If you purchased this book after the beginning date of the chart, please send your original receipt along with the UPC bar code from the cover to:

Optimum Performance Technologies
P.O. Box 2164
Roswell, GA 30075

We will then send you the months you need to complete your entire year of OPS times.

THE OPTIMUM PERFORMANCE SCHEDULE

1 JUNE 1994–31 MAY 1995

June 1994

	Midnight	End	Begin		End	Begin		End	Begin		End	Begin		End	Begin		End	Begin		End	Begin		End	Begin	Mid
1	M	200	200	F	500	500	E	1000	1000	F	1130	1130	M	230p	230p	F	530p	530p	E	1030p	1030p	F			
2	M	300	300	F	600	600	E	1100	1100	F	1230	1230	M	330p	330p	F	630p	630p	E	1130p	1130p	F			
3	F	1230a	1230a	M	330	330	F	630	630	E	1130	1130	F	130p	130p	M	430p	430p	F	730p	730p	O			
4	F	130	130	M	430	430	F	730	730	E	1230	1230	F	200p	200p	M	500p	500p	F	800p	800p	O			
5	O	130	130	M	530	530	F	830	830	E	130p	130p	F	300p	300p	M	600p	600p	F	900p	900p	O			
6	O	200	200	M	600	600	F	900	900	E	200p	200p	F	330p	330p	M	630p	630p	F	930p	930p	O			
7	O	230	230	F	400	400	M	700	700	F	1000	1000	E	300p	300p	F	430p	430p	M	730p	730p	F	1030p	1030p	O
8	O	330	330	F	430	430	M	730	730	F	1030	1030	E	330p	330p	F	500p	500p	M	800p	800p	F	1100p	1100p	O
9	O	400	400	F	530	530	M	830	830	F	1130	1130	E	430p	430p	F	530p	530p	M	830p	830p	F	1130p	1130p	O
10	O	430	430	F	600	600	M	900	900	F	1200	1200	E	500p	500p	F	630p	630p	M	930p	930p	F			
11	O	500	500	F	630	630	M	930	930	F	1230	1230	E	530p	530p	F	630p	630p	M	930p	930p	F			
12	F	1230a	1230a	O	500	500	F	700	700	M	1000	1000	F	100p	100p	E	600p	600p	F	730p	730p	M	1030p	1030p	F
13	F	100	100	O	600	600	F	730	730	M	1030	1030	F	130p	130p	E	630p	630p	F	800p	800p	M	1100p	1100p	F
14	F	130	130	O	630	630	F	830	830	M	1130	1130	F	230p	230p	E	730p	730p	F	900p	900p	M			
15	F	230	230	O	730	730	F	930	930	M	1230	1230	F	330p	330p	E	830p	830p	F	1000p	1000p	M			
16	M	1230a	1230a	F	330	330	O	830	830	F	1030	1030	M	130p	130p	F	430p	430p	E	930p	930p	F	1100p	1100p	M
17	M	130	130	F	430	430	E	930	930	F	1130	1130	M	230p	230p	F	530p	530p	E	1030p	1030p	F			
18	M	300	300	F	600	600	E	1100	1100	F	1230	1230	M	330p	330p	F	630p	630p	O	1130p	1130p	F			
19	F	100	100	M	400	400	F	700	700	E	1200	1200	F	130p	130p	M	430p	430p	F	730p	730p	O			
20	O	1230a	1230a	F	200	200	M	500	500	F	800	800	E	100p	100p	F	230p	230p	M	530p	530p	F	830p	830p	O
21	O	130	130	F	300	300	M	600	600	F	900	900	E	200p	200p	F	330p	330p	M	630p	630p	F	930p	930p	O
22	O	230	230	F	400	400	M	700	700	F	1000	1000	E	300p	300p	F	430p	430p	M	730p	730p	F	1030p	1030p	O
23	O	330	330	F	500	500	M	800	800	F	1100	1100	E	400p	400p	F	530p	530p	M	830p	830p	F	1130p	1130p	O
24	O	430	430	F	600	600	M	900	900	F	1200	1200	O	500p	500p	F	600p	600p	M	900p	900p	F			
25	O	500	500	F	630	630	M	930	930	F	1230	1230	O	530p	530p	F	700p	700p	M	1000p	1000p	F			
26	F	100	100	O	600	600	F	730	730	M	1030	1030	F	130p	130p	E	630p	630p	F	800p	800p	M	1100p	1100p	F
27	F	200	200	O	700	700	F	830	830	M	1130	1130	F	230p	230p	E	730p	730p	F	900p	900p	M			
28	F	230	230	O	730	730	F	900	900	M	1200	1200	F	300p	300p	E	800p	800p	F	930p	930p	M			
29	M	1230a	1230a	F	330	330	O	830	830	F	1000	1000	M	100p	100p	F	400p	400p	E	900p	900p	F	1030p	1030p	M
30	M	130	130	F	430	430	E	930	930	F	1100	1100	M	200p	200p	F	500p	500p	E	1000p	1000p	F	1130p	1130p	M

Locate the OPStime between the start and end times. For example on June 1, if you want to schedule your appointment in an Excellent Green time

look for the E for Excellent Green times and you will notice that it falls between a start time of 5am and and end time of 1000am. Schedule your appointment accordingly.

O is Optimum Gold | E is Excellent Green | M is Moderate Blue | F is Fair Red | Add one hour for Daylight Savings Time to times shown.

July 1994

	Midnight	End	Begin		End	Begin		End	Begin		End	Begin		End	Begin		End	Begin		End	Begin		End	Begin	Mid
1	M	200	200	F	500	500	E	1000	1000	F	1200	1200	M	300p	300p	F	600p	600p	E	1100p	1100p	F			
2	M	300	300	F	600	600	E	1100	1100	F	1230	1230	M	330p	330p	F	630p	630p	E	1130p	1130p	F			
3	F	100	100	M	400	400	F	700	700	E	1200	1200	F	130p	130p	M	430p	430p	F	730p	730p	O			
4	O	1230a	1230a	F	200	200	M	500	500	F	800	800	E	100p	100p	F	230p	230p	M	530p	530p	F	830p	830p	O
5	O	100	100	F	230	230	M	530	530	F	830	830	E	130p	130p	F	300p	300p	M	600p	600p	F	900p	900p	O
6	O	200	200	F	330	330	M	630	630	F	930	930	E	230p	230p	F	400p	400p	M	700p	700p	F	1000p	1000p	O
7	O	300	300	F	400	400	M	700	700	F	1000	1000	E	300p	300p	F	430p	430p	M	730p	730p	F	1030p	1030p	O
8	O	330	330	F	500	500	M	800	800	F	1100	1100	E	400p	400p	F	500p	500p	M	800p	800p	F	1100p	1100p	O
9	O	400	400	F	530	530	M	830	830	F	1130	1130	E	430p	430p	F	530p	530p	M	830p	830p	F	1130p	1130p	O
10	O	430	430	F	600	600	M	900	900	F	1200	1200	E	500p	500p	F	600p	600p	M	900p	900p	F			
11	O	500	500	F	630	630	M	930	930	F	1230	1230	E	530p	530p	F	700p	700p	M	1000p	1000p	F			
12	F	100	100	O	600	600	F	730	730	M	1030	1030	F	130p	130p	E	630p	630p	F	730p	730p	M	1030p	1030p	F
13	F	130	130	O	630	630	F	800	800	M	1100	1100	F	200p	200p	E	700p	700p	F	830p	830p	M	1130p	1130p	F
14	F	230	230	O	730	730	F	900	900	M	1200	1200	F	300p	300p	E	800p	800p	F	930p	930p	M			
15	M	30	30	F	330	330	O	830	830	F	1000	1000	M	100p	100p	F	400p	400p	O	900p	900p	F	1030p	1030p	M
16	M	130	130	F	430	430	E	930	930	F	1100	1100	M	200p	200p	F	500p	500p	E	1000p	1000p	F	1130p	1130p	M
17	M	230	230	F	530	530	E	1030	1030	F	1230	1230	M	330p	330p	F	630p	630p	O	1130p	1130p	F			
18	F	100	100	M	400	400	F	700	700	E	1200	1200	F	130p	130p	M	430p	430p	F	730p	730p	O			
19	O	1230a	1230a	F	200	200	M	500	500	F	800	800	E	100p	100p	F	230p	230p	M	530p	530p	F	830p	830p	O
20	O	130	130	F	300	300	M	600	600	F	900	900	E	200p	200p	F	330p	330p	M	630p	630p	F	930p	930p	O
21	O	230	230	F	400	400	M	700	700	F	1000	1000	E	300p	300p	F	400p	400p	M	700p	700p	F	1000p	1000p	O
22	O	300	300	F	430	430	M	730	730	F	1030	1030	O	330p	330p	F	500p	500p	M	800p	800p	F	1100p	1100p	O
23	O	400	400	F	530	530	M	830	830	F	1130	1130	O	430p	430p	F	600p	600p	M	900p	900p	F			
24	O	500	500	F	630	630	M	930	930	F	1230	1230	O	530p	530p	F	700p	700p	M	1000p	1000p	F			
25	F	1230a	1230a	O	500	500	F	700	700	M	1000	1000	F	100p	100p	E	600p	600p	F	730p	730p	M	1030p	1030p	F
26	F	130	130	O	630	630	F	800	800	M	1100	1100	F	200p	200p	E	700p	700p	F	830p	830p	M	1130p	1130p	F
27	F	200	200	O	700	700	F	830	830	M	1130	1130	F	230p	230p	E	730p	730p	F	900p	900p	M			
28	F	300	300	E	800	800	F	930	930	M	1230	1230	F	330p	330p	E	830p	830p	F	1000p	1000p	M			
29	M	1230a	1230a	F	330	330	E	830	830	F	1000	1000	M	100p	100p	F	400p	400p	E	900p	900p	F	1030p	1030p	M
30	M	130	130	F	430	430	E	930	930	F	1100	1100	M	200p	200p	F	500p	500p	E	1000p	1000p	F	1130p	1130p	M
31	M	230	230	F	530	530	E	1030	1030	F	1200	1200	M	300p	300p	F	600p	600p	E	1100p	1100p	F			

Locate the OPStime between the start and end times. For example on June 1, if you want to schedule your appointment in an Excellent Green time look for the E for Excellent Green times and you will notice that it falls between a start time of 5am and and end time of 1000am. Schedule your appointment accordingly.

O is Optimum Gold | E is Excellent Green | M is Moderate Blue | F is Fair Red | Add one hour for Daylight Savings Time to times shown.

August 1994

	Midnight	End	Begin		End	Begin		End	Begin		End	Begin		End	Begin		End	Begin		End	Begin		End	Begin	Mid
1	M	300	300	F	600	600	E	1100	1100	F	100p	100p	M	400p	400p	F	700p	700p	E	0					
2	F	100	100	M	400	400	F	700	700	E	1200	1200	F	130p	130p	M	430p	430p	F	730p	730p	E			
3	E	1230a	1230a	F	200	200	M	500	500	F	800	800	E	100p	100p	F	230p	230p	M	530p	530p	F	830p	830p	E
4	E	130	130	F	300	300	M	600	600	F	900	900	E	200p	200p	F	300p	300p	M	600p	600p	F	900p	900p	O
5	O	200	200	F	330	330	M	630	630	F	930	930	E	230p	230p	F	400p	400p	M	700p	700p	F	1000p	1000p	O
6	O	300	300	F	430	430	M	730	730	F	1030	1030	E	330p	330p	F	430p	430p	M	730p	730p	F	1030p	1030p	O
7	O	400	400	F	500	500	M	800	800	F	1100	1100	E	400p	400p	F	500p	500p	M	800p	800p	F		1100p	O
8	O	430	430	F	530	530	M	830	830	F	1130	1130	O	430p	430p	F	600p	600p	M	900p	900p	F			
9	O	500	500	F	630	630	M	930	930	F	1230	1230	O	530p	530p	F	700p	700p	M	1000p	1000p	F			
10	F	1230a	1230a	O	500	500	F	700	700	M	1000	1000	F	100p	100p	O	600p	600p	F	730p	730p	M	1030p	1030p	F
11	F	130	130	O	630	630	F	800	800	M	1100	1100	F	200p	200p	O	700p	700p	F	830p	830p	M	1130p	1130p	F
12	F	200	200	O	700	700	F	900	900	M	1200	1200	F	300p	300p	O	800p	800p	F	930p	930p	M			
13	F	300	300	E	800	800	F	1000	1000	M	1230	1230	F	400p	400p	O	900p	900p	F	1030p	1030p	M			
14	M	130	130	F	430	430	E	930	930	F	1100	1100	M	200p	200p	F	500p	500p	O	1000p	1000p	F	1130p	1130p	M
15	M	230	230	F	530	530	E	1030	1030	F	1200	1200	M	300p	300p	F	600p	600p	O	1100p	1100p	F			
16	F	1230a	1230a	M	330	330	F	630	630	E	1130	1130	F	100p	100p	M	400p	400p	F	700p	700p	O			
17	F	130	130	M	430	430	F	730	730	E	1230	1230	F	200p	200p	M	500p	500p	F	800p	800p	O			
18	O	100	100	F	230	230	M	530	530	F	830	830	E	130p	130p	F	300p	300p	M	600p	600p	F	900p	900p	O
19	O	200	200	F	330	330	M	630	630	F	930	930	O	230p	230p	F	400p	400p	M	700p	700p	F	1000p	1000p	O
20	O	300	300	F	430	430	M	730	730	F	1030	1030	O	330p	330p	F	430p	430p	M	730p	730p	F	1030p	1030p	O
21	O	330	330	F	500	500	M	800	800	F	1100	1100	O	400p	400p	F	530p	530p	M	830p	830p	F	1130p	1130p	O
22	O	430	430	F	600	600	M	900	900	F	1200	1200	O	500p	500p	F	630p	630p	M	930p	930p	F			
23	O	500	500	F	630	630	M	930	930	F	1230	1230	O	530p	530p	F	700p	700p	M	1000p	1000p	F			
24	F	100	100	O	600	600	F	730	730	M	1030	1030	F	130p	130p	E	630p	630p	F	800p	800p	M	1100p	1100p	F
25	F	130	130	E	630	630	F	800	800	M	1100	1100	F	200p	200p	E	700p	700p	F	830p	830p	M			
26	F	200	200	E	700	700	F	830	830	M	1130	1130	F	230p	230p	E	730p	730p	F	900p	900p	M			
27	F	300	300	E	800	800	F	930	930	M	1230	1230	F	330p	330p	E	830p	830p	F	1000p	1000p	M			
28	M	1230a	1230a	F	330	330	E	830	830	F	1000	1000	M	100p	100p	F	400p	400p	E	900p	900p	F	1030p	1030p	M
29	M	130	130	F	430	430	E	930	930	F	1100	1100	M	200p	200p	F	500p	500p	E	1000p	1000p	F	1130p	1130p	M
30	M	230	230	F	530	530	E	1030	1030	F	1200	1200	M	300p	300p	F	600p	600p	E	1100p	1100p	F			
31	F	1230a	1230a	M	330	330	F	630	630	E	1130	1130	F	100p	100p	M	400p	400p	F	700p	700p	E			

Locate the OPStime between the start and end times. For example on June 1, if you want to schedule your appointment in an Excellent Green time look for the E for Excellent Green times and you will notice that it falls between a start time of 5am and and end time of 1000am. Schedule your appointment accordingly.

O is Optimum Gold | E is Excellent Green | M is Moderate Blue | F is Fair Red | Add one hour for Daylight Savings Time to times shown.

September 1994

	Midnight	End	Begin		End	Begin		End	Begin		End	Begin		End	Begin		End	Begin		End	Begin		End	Begin	Mid
1	F	130	130	M	430	430	F	730	730	E	1230	1230	F	200p	200p	M	500p	500p	F	800p	800p	O			
2	O	100	100	F	200	200	M	500	500	F	800	800	E	100p	100p	F	230p	230p	M	530p	530p	F	830p	830p	O
3	O	130	130	F	300	300	M	600	600	F	900	900	E	200p	200p	F	330p	330p	M	630p	630p	F	930p	930p	O
4	O	230	230	F	350	350	M	650	650	F	950	950	O	1450	1450	F	400p	400p	M	700p	700p	F	1000p	1000p	O
5	O	300	300	F	430	430	M	730	730	F	1030	1030	O	330p	330p	F	500p	500p	M	800p	800p	F	1100p	1100p	O
6	O	400	400	F	530	530	M	830	830	F	1130	1130	O	430p	430p	F	530p	530p	M	830p	830p	F	1130p	1130p	O
7	O	430	430	F	600	600	M	900	900	F	1200	1200	O	500p	500p	F	630p	630p	M	930p	930p	F			
8	F	1230a	1230a	O	500	500	F	700	700	M	1000	1000	F	1300	1300	O	600p	600p	F	730	730	M	1030p	1030p	F
9	F	100	100	O	600	600	F	730	730	M	1030	1030	F	1330	1330	O	630p	630p	F	800p	800p	M	1100p	1100p	F
10	F	200	200	O	700	700	F	830	830	M	1130	1130	F	1430	1430	O	730p	730p	F	900p	900p	M			
11	F	300	300	E	800	800	F	930	930	M	1230	1230	F	330p	330p	O	830p	830p	F	1000p	1000p	M			
12	M	100	100	F	400	400	E	900	900	F	1100	1100	M	200p	200p	F	500p	500p	O	1000p	1000p	F	1130p	1130p	M
13	M	230	230	F	530	530	E	1030	1030	F	1200	1200	M	300p	300p	F	600p	600p	O	1100p	1100p	F			
14	F	1230a	1230a	M	330	330	F	630	630	E	1130	1130	F	100p	100p	M	400p	400p	F	700p	700p	O			
15	F	130	130	M	430	430	F	730	730	E	1230	1230	F	200p	200p	M	500p	500p	F	800p	800p	O			
16	O	100	100	F	230	230	M	530	530	F	830	830	E	130p	130p	F	300p	300p	M	600p	600p	F	900p	900p	O
17	O	130	130	F	300	300	M	600	600	F	900	900	O	200p	200p	F	330p	330p	M	630p	630p	F	930p	930p	O
18	O	230	230	F	400	400	M	700	700	F	1000	1000	O	300p	300p	F	430p	430p	M	730p	730p	F	1030p	1030p	O
19	O	330	330	F	500	500	M	800	800	F	1100	1100	O	400p	400p	F	500p	500p	M	800p	800p	F	1100p	1100p	O
20	O	400	400	F	530	530	M	830	830	F	1130	1130	O	430p	430p	F	530p	530p	M	830p	830p	F	1130p	1130p	O
21	O	430	430	F	600	600	M	900	900	F	1200	1200	O	500p	500p	F	630p	630p	M	930p	930p	F			
22	F	1230a	1230a	E	500	500	F	630	630	M	930	930	F	1230	1230	E	530p	530p	F	700p	700p	M	1000p	1000p	F
23	F	100	100	E	600	600	F	730	730	M	1030	1030	F	130p	130p	E	630p	630p	F	800p	800p	M	1100p	1100p	F
24	F	130	130	E	630	630	F	800	800	M	1100	1100	F	200p	200p	E	700p	700p	F	830p	830p	M	1130p	1130p	F
25	F	200	200	E	700	700	F	830	830	M	1130	1130	F	230p	230p	E	730p	730p	F	900p	900p	M			
26	F	230	230	E	730	730	F	900	900	M	1200	1200	F	300p	300p	E	800p	800p	F	930p	930p	M			
27	M	1230a	1230a	F	330	330	E	830	830	F	1000	1000	M	100p	100p	F	400p	400p	E	900p	900p	F	1030p	1030p	M
28	M	130	130	F	430	430	E	930	930	F	1100	1100	M	200p	200p	F	500p	500p	E	1000p	1000p	F	1130p	1130p	M
29	M	230	230	F	530	530	E	1030	1030	F	1200	1200	M	300p	300p	F	600p	600p	E	1100p	1100p	F			
30	F	1230a	1230a	M	330	330	F	630	630	E	1130	1130	F	100p	100p	M	400p	400p	F	700p	700p	E			

Locate the OPStime between the start and end times. For example on June 1, if you want to schedule your appointment in an Excellent Green time look for the E for Excellent Green times and you will notice that it falls between a start time of 5am and and end time of 1000am. Schedule your appointment accordingly.

O is Optimum Gold | E is Excellent Green | M is Moderate Blue | F is Fair Red | Add one hour for Daylight Savings Time to times shown.

October 1994

	Midnight	End	Begin		End	Begin		End	Begin		End	Begin		End	Begin		End	Begin		End	Begin		End	Begin	Mid
1	F	130	130	M	430	430	F	730	730	E	1230	1230	F	200p	200p	M	500p	500p	F	800p	800p	O			
2	O	100	100	F	230	230	M	530	530	F	830	830	E	130p	130p	F	300p	300p	M	600p	600p	F	900p	900p	O
3	O	200	200	F	330	330	M	630	630	F	930	930	E	230p	230p	F	330p	330p	M	630p	630p	F	930p	930p	O
4	O	230	230	F	400	400	M	700	700	F	1000	1000	O	300p	300p	F	430p	430p	M	730p	730p	F	1030p	1030p	O
5	O	330	330	F	500	500	M	800	800	F	1100	1100	O	400p	400p	F	530p	530p	M	830p	830p	F	1130p	1130p	O
6	O	430	430	F	530	530	M	830	830	F	1130	1130	O	430p	430p	F	600p	600p	M	900p	900p	F			
7	O	500	500	F	630	630	M	930	930	F	1230	1230	O	530p	530p	F	700p	700p	M	1000p	1000p	F			
8	F	100	100	O	600	600	F	730	730	M	1030	1030	F	130p	130p	O	630p	630p	F	800p	800p	M	1100p	1100p	F
9	F	200	200	E	700	700	F	830	830	M	1130	1130	F	230p	230p	O	730p	730p	F	900p	900p	M			
10	F	250	250	E	750	750	F	1030	1030	M	1230	1230	F	330p	330p	O	830p	830p	F	1000p	1000p	M			
11	M	100	100	F	400	400	E	900	900	F	1030	1030	M	130p	130p	F	430p	430p	O	930p	930p	F			
12	M	200	200	F	500	500	E	1000	1000	F	1130	1130	M	230p	230p	F	530p	530p	E	1030p	1030p	F			
13	M	300	300	F	600	600	E	1100	1100	F	1230	1230	M	330p	330p	F	630p	630p	E	1130p	1130p	F			
14	F	100	100	M	400	400	F	700	700	E	1200	1200	F	130p	130p	M	430p	430p	F	730p	730p	O			
15	O	1230a	1230a	F	200	200	M	500	500	F	800	800	E	100p	100p	F	230p	230p	M	530p	530p	F	830p	830p	E
16	O	130	130	F	250	250	M	550	550	F	850	850	O	1350	1350	F	300p	300p	M	600p	600p	F	900p	900p	O
17	O	200	200	F	330	330	M	630	630	F	930	930	O	230p	230p	F	400p	400p	M	700p	700p	F	1000p	1000p	O
18	O	300	300	F	430	430	M	730	730	F	1030	1030	O	330p	330p	F	430p	430p	M	730p	730p	F	1030p	1030p	O
19	O	330	330	F	500	500	M	800	800	F	1100	1100	O	400p	400p	F	530p	530p	M	830p	830p	F	1130p	1130p	E
20	E	430	430	F	530	530	M	830	830	F	1130	1130	O	430p	430p	F	600p	600p	M	900p	900p	F			
21	E	500	500	F	600	600	M	900	900	F	1200	1200	E	500p	500p	F	630p	630p	M	930p	930p	F			
22	F	1230a	1230a	E	500	500	F	700	700	M	1000	1000	F	100p	100p	E	600p	600p	F	700p	700p	M	1000p	1000p	F
23	F	100	100	E	600	600	F	700	700	M	1000	1000	F	100p	100p	E	600p	600p	F	730p	730p	M	1030p	1030p	F
24	F	130	130	E	630	630	F	730	730	M	1030	1030	F	130p	130p	E	630p	630p	F	800p	800p	M	1100p	1100p	F
25	F	200	200	E	700	700	F	830	830	M	1130	1130	F	230p	230p	E	730p	730p	F	830p	830p	M	1130p	1130p	F
26	F	230	230	E	730	730	F	900	900	M	1200	1200	F	300p	300p	E	800p	800p	F	930p	930p	M			
27	M	1230a	1230a	F	330	330	E	830	830	F	1000	1000	M	100p	100p	F	400p	400p	E	900p	900p	F	1030p	1030p	M
28	M	130	130	F	430	430	E	930	930	F	1100	1100	M	200p	200p	F	500p	500p	E	1000p	1000p	F	1130p	1130p	M
29	M	230	230	F	530	530	E	1030	1030	F	1200	1200	M	300p	300p	F	600p	600p	E	1100p	1100p	F			
30	F	100	100	M	400	400	F	700	700	E	1200	1200	F	130p	130p	M	430p	430p	F	730p	730p	E			
31	E	1230a	1230a	F	200	200	M	500	500	F	800	800	E	100p	100p	F	230p	230p	M	530p	530p	F	830p	830p	E

Locate the OPStime between the start and end times. For example on June 1, if you want to schedule your appointment in an Excellent Green time look for the E for Excellent Green times and you will notice that it falls between a start time of 5am and and end time of 1000am. Schedule your appointment accordingly.

O is Optimum Gold | E is Excellent Green | M is Moderate Blue | F is Fair Red | Add one hour for Daylight Savings Time to times shown.

November 1994

	Midnight	End	Begin		End	Begin		End	Begin		End	Begin		End	Begin		End	Begin		End	Begin		End	Begin	Mid
1	E	130	130	F	230	230	M	530	530	F	830	830	O	130p	130p	F	300p	300p	M	600p	600p	F	900p	900p	O
2	O	200	200	F	330	330	M	630	630	F	930	930	O	230p	230p	F	400p	400p	M	700p	700p	F	1000p	1000p	O
3	O	300	300	F	430	430	M	730	730	F	1030	1030	O	330p	330p	F	500p	500p	M	800p	800p	F	1100p	1100p	O
4	O	400	400	F	530	530	M	830	830	F	1130	1130	O	430p	430p	F	600p	600p	M	900p	900p	F			
5	O	500	500	F	630	630	M	930	930	F	1230	1230	O	530p	530p	F	630p	630p	M	930p	930p	F			
6	F	1230a	1230a	E	500	500	F	700	700	M	1000	1000	F	100p	100p	O	600p	600p	F	730p	730p	M			
7	F	130	130	O	630	630	F	800	800	M	1100	1100	F	200p	200p	O	700p	700p	F	830p	830p	M			
8	F	230	230	E	730	730	F	900	900	M	1200	1200	F	300p	300p	O	800p	800p	F	930p	930p	M			
9	M	1230a	1230a	F	330	330	E	830	830	F	1000	1000	M	100p	100p	F	400p	400p	O	900p	900p	F	1030p	1030p	M
10	M	130	130	F	430	430	E	930	930	F	1100	1100	M	200p	200p	F	500p	500p	E	1000p	1000p	F	1130p	1130p	M
11	M	230	230	F	530	530	E	1030	1030	F	1200	1200	M	300p	300p	F	600p	600p	E	1100p	1100p	F			
12	F	1230a	1230a	M	330	330	F	630	630	E	1130	1130	F	100p	100p	M	400p	400p	F	700p	700p	E			
13	F	130	130	M	430	430	F	730	730	E	1230	1230	F	200p	200p	M	500p	500p	F	800p	800p	E			
14	E	100	100	F	230	230	M	530	530	F	830	830	O	130p	130p	F	230p	230p	M	530p	530p	F	830p	830p	O
15	O	130	130	F	300	300	M	600	600	F	900	900	O	200p	200p	F	330p	330p	M	630p	630p	F	930p	930p	E
16	E	200	200	F	400	400	M	700	700	F	1000	1000	O	300p	300p	F	400p	400p	M	700p	700p	F	1000p	1000p	E
17	E	300	300	F	430	430	M	730	730	F	1030	1030	O	330p	330p	F	500p	500p	M	800p	800p	F	1100p	1100p	E
18	E	400	400	F	500	500	M	800	800	F	1100	1100	O	400p	400p	F	530p	530p	M	830p	830p	F	1130p	1130p	E
19	E	430	430	F	600	600	M	900	900	F	1200	1200	O	500p	500p	F	600p	600p	M	900p	900p	F			
20	E	500	500	F	630	630	M	930	930	F	1230	1230	E	530p	530p	F	630p	630p	M	930p	930p	F			
21	F	1230a	1230a	E	500	500	F	630	630	M	930	930	F	1230	1230	E	530p	530p	F	700p	700p	M			
22	F	100	100	E	600	600	F	700	700	M	1000	1000	F	100p	100p	E	600p	600p	F	730p	730p	M			
23	F	130	130	E	630	630	F	800	800	M	1100	1100	F	200p	200p	E	700p	700p	F	800p	800p	M			
24	F	200	200	E	700	700	F	830	830	M	1130	1130	F	230p	230p	E	730p	730p	F	900p	900p	M			
25	F	300	300	E	800	800	F	930	930	M	1230	1230	F	330p	330p	E	830p	830p	F	1000p	1000p	M			
26	M	100	100	F	400	400	E	900	900	F	1030	1030	M	130p	130p	F	430p	430p	E	930p	930p	F	1100p	1100p	M
27	M	200	200	F	500	500	E	1000	1000	F	1130	1130	M	230p	230p	F	530p	530p	E	1030p	1030p	F			
28	F	1230a	1230a	M	330	330	F	630	630	E	1130	1130	F	1230	1230	M	330p	330p	F	630p	630p	E			
29	E	1230a	1230a	F	130	130	M	430	430	F	730	730	O	1230	1230	F	200p	200p	M	500p	500p	F	800p	800p	E
30	E	100	100	F	230	230	M	530	530	F	830	830	O	130p	130p	F	300p	300p	M	600p	600p	F	900p	900p	O

Locate the OPStime between the start and end times. For example on June 1, if you want to schedule your appointment in an Excellent Green time look for the E for Excellent Green times and you will notice that it falls between a start time of 5am and and end time of 1000am. Schedule your appointment accordingly.

O is Optimum Gold | E is Excellent Green | M is Moderate Blue | F is Fair Red

Decemeber 1994

Day	Midnight	End	Begin		End	Begin		End	Begin		End	Begin		End	Begin		End	Begin		End	Begin		End	Begin	Mid
1	O	200	200	F	330	330	M	630	630	F	930	930	O	230p	230p	F	400p	400p	M	700p	700p	F	1000p	1000p	O
2	E	300	300	F	430	430	M	730	730	F	1030	1030	O	330p	330p	F	500p	500p	M	800p	800p	F	1100p	1100p	E
3	E	400	400	F	500	500	M	800	800	F	1100	1100	O	400p	400p	F	530p	530p	M	830p	830p	F	1130p	1130p	O
4	O	430	430	F	600	600	M	900	900	F	1200	1200	O	500p	500p	F	630p	630p	M	930p	930p	F			
5	F	1230a	1230a	O	500	500	F	700	700	M	1000	1000	F	100p	100p	O	600p	600p	F	730p	730p	M			
6	F	130	130	O	630	630	F	800	800	M	1100	1100	F	200p	200p	O	700p	700p	F	830p	830p	M			
7	F	230	230	E	730	730	F	830	830	M	1130	1130	F	230p	230p	O	730p	730p	F	930p	930p	M			
8	M	1230a	1230a	F	330	330	E	830	830	F	930	930	M	1230	1230	F	330p	330p	O	830p	830p	F	1000p	1000p	M
9	M	100	100	F	400	400	E	900	900	F	1030	1030	M	130p	130p	F	430p	430p	E	930p	930p	F	1100p	1100p	M
10	M	200	200	F	500	500	E	1000	1000	F	1130	1130	M	230p	230p	F	530p	530p	E	1030p	1030p	F			
11	M	300	300	F	600	600	E	1100	1100	F	1230	1230	M	330p	330p	F	630p	630p	E	1130p	1130p	F			
12	F	100	100	M	400	400	F	700	700	E	1200	1200	F	130p	130p	M	430	430	F	730p	730p	E			
13	E	1230am	1230am	F	200	200	M	500	500	F	800	800	O	100p	100p	F	200p	200p	M	500p	500p	F	800p	800p	E
14	E	100	100	F	230	230	M	530	530	F	830	830	O	130p	130p	F	300p	300p	M	600p	600p	F	900p	900p	E
15	E	200	200	F	330	330	M	630	630	F	930	930	O	230p	230p	F	330p	330p	M	630p	630p	F	930p	930p	E
16	E	230	230	F	400	400	M	700	700	F	1000	1000	O	300p	300p	F	430p	430p	M	730p	730p	F	1030p	1030p	E
17	E	330	330	F	500	500	M	800	800	F	1100	1100	O	400p	400p	F	500p	500p	M	800p	800p	F	1100p	1100p	E
18	E	400	400	F	530	530	M	830	830	F	1130	1130	O	430p	430p	F	530p	530p	M	830p	830p	F	1130p	1130p	E
19	E	430	430	F	600	600	M	900	900	F	1200	1200	O	500p	500p	F	600p	600p	M	900p	900p	F			E
20	E	500	500	F	630	630	M	930	930	F	1230	1230	O	530p	530p	F	630p	630p	M	930p	930p	F			
21	F	1230a	1230a	E	500	500	F	700	700	M	1000	1000	F	100p	100p	E	600p	600p	F	700p	700p	M			
22	F	100	100	E	600	600	F	730	730	M	1030	1030	F	130p	130p	E	630p	630p	F	800p	800p	M			
23	F	200	200	E	700	700	F	800	800	M	1100	1100	F	200p	200p	E	700p	700p	F	830p	830p	M			
24	F	230	230	E	730	730	F	900	900	M	1200	1200	F	300p	300p	E	800p	800p	F	930p	930p	M			
25	M	1230a	1230a	F	330	330	E	830	830	F	1000	1000	M	100p	100p	F	400p	400p	E	900p	900p	F	1030p	1030p	M
26	M	130	130	F	430	430	E	930	930	F	1100	1100	M	200p	200p	F	500p	500p	E	1000p	1000p	F			
27	M	300	300	F	600	600	E	1100	1100	F	1230	1230	M	330p	330p	F	630p	630p	E	1130p	1130p	F			
28	F	100	100	M	400	400	F	700	700	O	1200	1200	F	130p	130p	M	430p	430p	F	730p	730p	E			
29	E	1230a	1230a	F	200	200	M	500	500	F	800	800	O	100p	100p	F	230p	230p	M	530p	530p	F	830p	830p	E
30	E	130	130	F	300	300	M	600	600	F	900	900	E	200p	200p	F	330p	330p	M	630p	630p	F	930p	930p	O
31	O	230	230	F	400	400	M	700	700	F	1000	1000	O	300p	300p	F	430p	430p	M	730p	730p	F	1030p	1030p	E

Locate the OPStime between the start and end times. For example on June 1, if you want to schedule your appointment in an Excellent Green time look for the E for Excellent Green times and you will notice that it falls between a start time of 5am and and end time of 1000am. Schedule your appointment accordingly.

O is Optimum Gold | E is Excellent Green | M is Moderate Blue | F is Fair Red | Add one hour for Daylight Savings Time to times shown.

January 1995

	Midnight	End	Begin		End	Begin		End	Begin		End	Begin		End	Begin		End	Begin		End	Begin		End	Begin	Mid
1	E	330	330	F	500	500	M	800	800	F	1100	1100	O	400p	400p	F	530p	530p	M	830p	830p	F	1130p	1130p	O
2	O	430	430	F	600	600	M	900	900	F	1200	1200	O	500p	500p	F	600p	600p	M	900p	900p	F			
3	O	500	500	F	630	630	M	930	930	F	1230	1230	O	530p	530p	F	700p	700p	M	1000p	1000p	F			
4	F	100	100	O	600	600	F	730	730	M	1030	1030	F	130p	130p	O	630p	630p	F	800p	800p	M			
5	F	200	200	O	700	700	F	800	800	M	1100	1100	F	200p	200p	O	700p	700p	F	900p	900p	M			
6	F	300	300	E	800	800	F	900	900	M	1200	1200	F	300p	300p	O	800p	800p	F	930p	930p	M			
7	M	1230a	1230a	F	330	330	E	830	830	F	1000	1000	M	100p	100p	F	400p	400p	E	900p	900p	F	1030p	1030p	M
8	M	130	130	F	430	430	E	930	930	F	1100	1100	M	200p	200p	F	500p	500p	E	1000p	1000p	F	1130p	1130p	M
9	M	230	230	F	530	530	E	1030	1030	F	1200	1200	M	300p	300p	F	600p	600p	E	1100p	1100p	F			
10	F	1230a	1230a	M	330	330	F	630	630	E	1130	1130	F	1230	1230	M	330p	330p	F	630p	630p	E	1130p	1130p	F
11	F	100	100	M	400	400	F	700	700	E	1200	1200	F	130p	130p	M	430p	430p	F	730p	730p	E			
12	E	1230am	1230am	F	200	200	M	500	500	F	800	800	E	100p	100p	F	230p	230p	M	530p	530p	F	830p	830p	E
13	E	130	130	F	300	300	M	600	600	F	900	900	O	200p	200p	F	300p	300p	M	600p	600p	F	900p	900p	E
14	E	200	200	F	330	330	M	630	630	F	930	930	O	230p	230p	F	400p	400p	M	700p	700p	F	1000p	1000p	E
15	E	300	300	F	430	430	M	730	730	F	1030	1030	O	330p	330p	F	430p	430p	M	730p	730p	F	1030p	1030p	E
16	E	330	330	F	500	500	M	800	800	F	1100	1100	O	400p	400p	F	530p	530p	M	830p	830p	F	1130p	1130p	E
17	E	430	430	F	530	530	M	830	830	F	1130	1130	O	430p	430p	F	600p	600p	M	900p	900p	F			
18	E	500	500	F	600	600	M	900	900	F	1200	1200	O	500p	500p	F	630p	630p	M	930p	930p	F			
19	F	1230a	1230a	E	500	500	F	630	630	M	930	930	F	1230	1230	O	530p	530p	F	700p	700p	M			
20	F	100	100	E	600	600	F	700	700	M	1000	1000	F	100p	100p	O	600p	600p	F	730p	730p	M			
21	F	130	130	E	630	630	F	800	800	M	1100	1100	F	200p	200p	E	700p	700p	F	830p	830p	M			
22	F	230	230	E	730	730	F	830	830	M	1130	1130	F	230p	230p	E	730p	730p	F	930p	930p	M			
23	M	1230a	1230a	F	330	330	E	830	830	F	930	930	M	1230	1230	F	330p	330p	E	830p	830p	F	1030p	1030p	M
24	M	130	130	F	430	430	E	930	930	F	1100	1100	M	200p	200p	F	500p	500p	E	1000p	1000p	F	1130p	1130p	M
25	M	230	230	F	530	530	E	1030	1030	F	1200	1200	M	300p	300p	F	600p	600p	E	1100p	1100p	F			
26	F	1230a	1230a	M	330	330	F	630	630	E	1130	1130	F	130p	130p	M	430p	430p	F	730p	730p	E			
27	E	1230am	1230am	F	200	200	M	500	500	F	800	800	O	100p	100p	F	230p	230p	M	530p	530p	F	830p	830p	E
28	E	130	130	F	300	300	M	600	600	F	900	900	O	200p	200p	F	330p	330p	M	630p	630p	F	930p	930p	O
29	O	230	230	F	400	400	M	700	700	F	1000	1000	O	300p	300p	F	400p	400p	M	700p	700p	F	1000p	1000p	O
30	O	300	300	F	430	430	M	730	730	F	1030	1030	O	330p	330p	F	500p	500p	M	800p	800p	F	1100p	1100p	O
31	O	400	400	F	530	530	M	830	830	F	1130	1130	O	430p	430p	F	600p	600p	M	900p	900p	F			

Locate the OPStime between the start and end times. For example on June 1, if you want to schedule your appointment in an Excellent Green time look for the E for Excellent Green times and you will notice that it falls between a start time of 5am and and end time of 1000am. Schedule your appointment accordingly.

O is Optimum Gold | E is Excellent Green | M is Moderate Blue | F is Fair Red

February 1995

Midnight		End	Begin		End	Begin		End	Begin		End	Begin		End	Begin		End	Begin		End	Begin		End	Begin	Mid
1	O	500	500	F	600	600	M	900	900	F	1200	1200	O	500p	500p	F	630p	630p	M	930p	930p	F			
2	F	1230a	1230a	O	500	500	F	700	700	M	1000	1000	F	100p	100p	O	600p	600p	F	730p	730p	M			
3	F	130	130	O	630	630	F	730	730	M	1030	1030	F	130p	130p	O	630p	630p	F	800p	800p	M			
4	F	200	200	O	700	700	F	830	830	M	1130	1130	F	230p	230p	E	730p	730p	F	900p	900p	M			
5	F	300	300	E	800	800	F	930	930	M	1230	1230	F	330p	330p	E	830p	830p	F	1000p	1000p	M			
6	M	100	100	F	400	400	E	900	900	F	1000	1000	M	100p	100p	F	400p	400p	E	900p	900p	F	1030p	1030p	M
7	M	130	130	F	430	430	E	930	930	F	1100	1100	M	200p	200p	F	500p	500p	E	1000p	1000p	F	1130p	1130p	M
8	M	230	230	F	530	530	E	1030	1030	F	1200	1200	M	300p	300p	F	600p	600p	E	1100p	1100p	F			
9	F	1230a	1230a	M	330	330	F	630	630	E	1130	1130	F	100p	100p	M	400p	400p	F	700p	700p	E			F
10	F	130	130	M	430	430	F	730	730	E	1230	1230	F	130p	130p	M	430p	430p	F	730p	730p	E			
11	E	1230am	1230am	F	200	200	M	500	500	F	800	800	E	100p	100p	F	230p	230p	M	530p	530p	F	830p	830p	E
12	E	130	130	F	300	300	M	600	600	F	900	900	O	200p	200p	F	330p	330p	M	630p	630p	F	930p	930p	E
13	E	230	230	F	400	400	M	700	700	F	1000	1000	O	300p	300p	F	400p	400p	M	700p	700p	F	1000p	1000p	E
14	E	300	300	F	430	430	M	730	730	F	1030	1030	O	330p	330p	F	500p	500p	M	800p	800p	F	1100p	1100p	E
15	E	400	400	F	500	500	M	800	800	F	1100	1100	O	400p	400p	F	530p	530p	M	830p	830p	F	1130p	1130p	O
16	O	430	430	F	530	530	M	830	830	F	1130	1130	O	430p	430p	F	600p	600p	M	900p	900p	F			
17	O	500	500	F	600	600	M	900	1200	O	1200	1200	O	500p	500p	F	630p	630p	M	930p	930p	F			
18	F	1230a	1230a	O	530	500	F	930	930	M	1230	1230	O	530p	530p	F	700p	700p	M	1000p	1000p	M			
19	F	130	130	O	630	630	F	730	730	M	1030	1030	F	130p	130p	E	630p	630p	F	800p	800p	M			
20	F	200	200	O	700	700	F	830	830	M	1130	1130	F	230p	230p	E	730p	730p	F	900p	900p	M			
21	F	300	300	O	800	800	F	930	930	M	1230	1230	F	330p	330p	E	830p	830p	F	1000p	1000p	M			
22	M	100	100	F	400	400	E	900	900	F	1030	1030	M	130p	130p	F	430p	430p	E	930p	930p	F	1130p	1130p	M
23	M	230	230	F	530	530	E	1030	1030	F	1200	1200	M	300p	300p	F	600p	600p	E	1100p	1100p	F			
24	F	1230a	1230a	M	330	330	F	630	630	E	1130	1130	F	100p	100p	M	400p	400p	F	700p	700p	E			
25	F	130	130	M	430	430	F	730	730	O	1230	1230	F	200p	200p	M	500p	500p	F	800p	800p	E			
26	E	100	100	F	230	230	M	530	530	F	830	830	O	130p	130p	F	300p	300p	M	600p	600p	F	900p	900p	O
27	O	200	200	F	330	330	M	630	630	F	930	930	O	230p	230p	F	400p	400p	M	700p	700p	F	1000p	1000p	O
28	O	300	300	F	430	430	M	730	730	F	1030	1030	O	330p	330p	F	500p	500p	M	800p	800p	F	1100p	1100p	O

Locate the OPStime between the start and end times. For example on June 1, if you want to schedule your appointment in an Excellent Green time look for the E for Excellent Green times and you will notice that it falls between a start time of 5am and and end time of 1000am. Schedule your appointment accordingly.

O is Optimum Gold | E is Excellent Green | M is Moderate Blue | F is Fair Red

March 1995

Midnight		End	Begin		End	Begin		End	Begin		End	Begin		End	Begin		End	Begin		End	Begin		End	Begin	Mid
1	O	400	400	F	500	500	M	800	800	F	1100	1100	O	400p	400p	F	530p	530p	M	830p	830p	F	1130p	1130p	O
2	O	430	430	F	600	600	M	900	900	F	1200	1200	O	500p	500p	F	630p	630p	M	930p	930p	F			
3	F	1230a	1230a	O	500	500	F	630	630	M	930	930	F	1230	1230	O	530p	530p	F	700p	700p	M			
4	F	100	100	O	600	600	F	730	730	M	1030	1030	F	130p	130p	E	630p	630p	F	730p	730p	M			
5	F	130	130	O	630	630	F	800	800	M	1100	1100	F	200p	200p	E	700p	700p	F	830p	830p	M			
6	F	230	230	E	730	730	F	830	830	M	1130	1130	F	230p	230p	E	730p	730p	F	900p	900p	M			
7	F	300	300	E	800	800	F	930	930	M	1230	1230	F	330p	330p	E	830p	830p	F	1000p	1000p	M			
8	M	100	100	F	400	400	E	900	900	F	1030	1030	M	130p	130p	F	430p	430p	E	930p	930p	F	1030p	1030p	M
9	M	130	130	F	430	430	E	930	930	F	1130	1130	M	230p	230p	F	530p	530p	E	1030p	1030p	F	1130p	1130p	M
10	M	230	230	F	530	530	E	1030	1030	F	1200	1200	M	300p	300p	F	600p	600p	E	1100p	1100p	F			
11	F	1230a	1230a	M	330	330	F	630	630	E	1130	1130	F	100p	100p	M	400p	400p	F	700p	700p	E			
12	F	130	130	M	430	430	F	730	730	E	1230	1230	F	200p	200p	M	500p	500p	F	800p	800p	E			
13	E	100	100	F	230	230	M	530	530	F	830	830	E	130p	130p	F	300p	300p	M	600p	600p	F	900p	900p	E
14	E	200	200	F	300	300	M	600	600	F	900	900	O	200p	200p	F	330p	330p	M	630p	630p	F	930p	930p	E
15	E	230	230	F	400	400	M	700	700	F	1000	1000	O	300p	300p	F	430p	430p	M	730p	730p	F	1030p	1030p	O
16	O	330	330	F	430	430	M	730	730	F	1030	1030	O	330p	330p	F	500p	500p	M	800p	800p	F	1100p	1100p	O
17	O	400	400	F	530	530	M	830	830	F	1130	1130	O	430p	430p	F	530p	530p	M	830p	830p	F	1130p	1130p	O
18	O	430	430	F	600	600	M	900	900	F	1200	1200	O	500p	500p	F	630p	630p	M	930p	930p	F			
19	F	1230a	1230a	O	500	500	F	630	630	M	930	930	F	1230	1230	O	530p	530p	F	700p	700p	M			
20	F	100	100	O	600	600	F	730	730	M	1030	1030	F	130p	130p	O	630p	630p	F	800p	800p	M			
21	F	200	200	O	700	700	F	830	830	M	1130	1130	F	230p	230p	E	730p	730p	F	900p	900p	M			
22	F	300	300	O	800	800	F	930	930	M	1230	1230	F	330p	330p	E	830p	830p	F	1000p	1000p	M			
23	M	100	100	F	400	400	O	900	900	F	1030	1030	M	130p	130p	F	430p	430p	E	930p	930p	F	1100p	1100p	M
24	M	200	200	F	500	500	E	1000	1000	F	1200	1200	M	300p	300p	F	600p	600p	E	1100p	1100p	F			
25	F	1230a	1230a	M	330	330	F	630	630	E	1130	1130	F	100p	100p	M	400p	400p	F	700p	700p	E			
26	F	130	130	M	430	430	F	730	730	O	1230	1230	F	200p	200p	M	500p	500p	F	800p	800p	E			
27	E	100	100	F	230	230	M	530	530	F	830	830	O	130p	130p	F	300p	300p	M	600p	600p	F	900p	900p	O
28	O	200	200	F	300	300	M	600	600	F	900	900	O	200p	200p	F	330p	330p	M	630p	630p	F	930p	930p	O
29	O	230	230	F	400	400	M	700	700	F	1000	1000	O	300p	300p	F	430p	430p	M	730p	730p	F	1030p	1030p	O
30	O	330	330	F	430	430	M	730	730	F	1030	1030	O	330p	330p	F	500p	500p	M	800p	800p	F	1100p	1100p	O
31	O	400	400	F	530	530	M	830	830	F	1130	1130	O	430p	430p	F	600p	600p	M	900p	900p	F			

Locate the OPStime between the start and end times. For example on June 1, if you want to schedule your appointment in an Excellent Green time look for the E for Excellent Green times and you will notice that it falls between a start time of 5am and and end time of 1000am. Schedule your appointment accordingly.

O is Optimum Gold | E is Excellent Green | M is Moderate Blue | F is Fair Red

April 1995

	Midnight	End	Begin		End	Begin		End	Begin		End	Begin		End	Begin		End	Begin		End	Begin		End	Begin	Mid
1	O	500	500	F	600	600	M	900	900	F	1200	1200	E	500p	500p	F	630p	630p	M	930p	930p	F			
2	F	1230a	1230a	O	500	500	F	700	700	M	1000	1000	F	100p	100p	E	600p	600p	F	700p	700p	M			
3	F	100	100	O	600	600	F	730	730	M	1030	1030	F	130p	130p	E	630p	630p	F	730p	730p	M			
4	F	130	130	O	630	630	F	800	800	M	1100	1100	F	200p	200p	E	700p	700p	F	830p	830p	M			
5	F	230	230	E	730	730	F	900	900	M	1200	1200	F	300p	300p	E	800p	800p	F	900p	900p	M			
6	F	300	300	E	800	800	F	930	930	M	1230	1230	F	330p	330p	E	830p	830p	F	930p	930p	M			
7	M	1230a	1230a	F	330	330	E	830	830	F	1030	1030	M	130p	130p	F	430p	430p	E	930p	930p	F	1030p	1030p	M
8	M	130	130	F	430	430	E	930	930	F	1130	1130	M	230p	230p	F	530p	530p	E	1030p	1030p	F	1130p	1130p	M
9	M	230	230	F	530	530	E	1030	1030	F	1230	1230	M	330p	330p	F	630p	630p	E	1130p	1130p	F			
10	F	1230a	1230a	M	330	330	F	630	630	E	1130	1130	F	130p	130p	M	430p	430p	F	730p	730p	E			
11	E	1230am	1230am	F	130	130	M	430	430	F	730	730	E	1230	1230	F	200p	200p	M	500p	500p	F	800p	800p	E
12	E	100	100	F	230	230	M	530	530	F	830	830	O	130p	130p	F	300p	300p	M	600p	600p	F	900p	900p	O
13	O	200	200	F	330	330	M	630	630	F	930	930	O	230p	230p	F	400p	400p	M	700p	700p	F	1000p	1000p	O
14	O	230	230	F	400	400	M	700	700	F	1000	1000	O	300p	300p	F	400p	400p	M	700p	700p	F	1030p	1030p	O
15	O	330	330	F	500	500	M	800	800	F	1100	1100	O	400p	400p	F	530p	530p	M	830p	830p	F	1130p	1130p	O
16	O	430	430	F	530	530	M	830	830	F	1130	1130	O	430p	430p	F	600p	600p	M	900p	900p	F			
17	O	500	500	F	630	630	M	930	930	F	1230	1230	O	530p	530p	F	700p	700p	M	1000p	1000p	F			
18	F	100	100	O	600	600	F	730	730	M	1030	1030	F	130p	130p	E	630p	630p	F	800p	800p	M			
19	F	200	200	O	700	700	F	830	830	M	1130	1130	F	230p	230p	E	730p	730p	F	830p	830p	M			
20	F	230	230	O	730	730	F	930	930	M	1230	1230	F	330p	330p	E	830p	830p	F	1000p	1000p	M			
21	M	100	100	F	400	400	O	900	900	F	1030	1030	M	130p	130p	F	430p	430p	E	930p	930p	F	1100p	1100p	M
22	M	200	200	F	500	500	O	1000	1000	F	1130	1130	M	230p	230p	F	530p	530p	E	1030p	1030p	F			
23	M	300	300	F	600	600	O	1100	1100	F	1230	1230	M	330p	330p	F	630p	630p	E	1130p	1130p	F			
24	F	100	100	M	400	400	F	700	700	O	1200	1200	F	130p	130p	M	430p	430p	F	730p	730p	O			
25	O	1230am	1230am	F	200	200	M	500	500	F	800	800	O	100p	100p	F	230p	230p	M	530p	530p	F	830p	830p	O
26	O	130	130	F	300	300	M	600	600	F	900	900	O	200p	200p	F	330p	330p	M	630p	630p	F	930p	930p	O
27	O	230	230	F	330	330	M	630	630	F	930	930	O	230p	230p	F	400p	400p	M	700p	700p	F	1000p	1000p	O
28	O	300	300	F	430	430	M	730	730	F	1030	1030	O	330p	330p	F	430p	430p	M	730p	730p	F	1030p	1030p	O
29	E	330	330	F	500	500	M	800	800	F	1100	1100	E	400p	400p	F	530p	530p	M	830p	830p	F	1130p	1130p	O
30	O	430	430	F	530	530	M	830	830	F	1130	1130	E	430p	430p	F	600p	600p	M	900p	900p	F			

Locate the OPStime between the start and end times. For example on June 1, if you want to schedule your appointment in an Excellent Green time look for the E for Excellent Green times and you will notice that it falls between a start time of 5am and and end time of 1000am. Schedule your appointment accordingly.

O is Optimum Gold | E is Excellent Green | M is Moderate Blue | F is Fair Red | Add one hour for Daylight Savings Time to times shown.

May 1995

Midnight		End	Begin		End	Begin		End	Begin		End	Begin		End	Begin		End	Begin		End	Begin		End	Begin	Mid
1	O	500	500	F	630	630	M	930	930	F	1230	1230	E	530p	530p	F	630p	630p	M	930p	930p	F			
2	F	1230a	1230a	O	500	500	F	700	700	M	1000	1000	F	100p	100p	E	600p	600p	F	700p	700p	M			
3	F	100	100	O	600	600	F	730	730	M	1030	1030	F	130p	130p	E	630p	630p	F	730p	730p	M			
4	F	130	130	E	630	630	F	800	800	M	1100	1100	F	200p	200p	E	700p	700p	F	800p	800p	M			
5	F	200	200	E	700	700	F	900	900	M	1200	1200	F	300p	300p	E	800p	800p	F	900p	900p	M			
6	F	300	300	E	800	800	F	930	930	M	1230	1230	F	330p	330p	E	830p	830p	F	930p	930p	M			
7	M	1230a	1230a	F	330	330	E	830	830	F	1030	1030	M	130p	130p	F	430p	430p	E	930p	930p	F	1030p	1030p	M
8	M	130	130	F	430	430	E	930	930	F	1130	1130	M	230p	230p	F	530p	530p	E	1030p	1030p	F	1130p	1130p	M
9	M	230	230	F	530	530	E	1030	1030	F	1230	1230	M	330p	330p	F	630p	630p	E	1130p	1130p	F			
10	F	100	100	M	400	400	F	700	700	E	1200	1200	F	130p	130p	M	430p	430p	F	730p	730p	E			
11	E	1230am	1230am	F	200	200	M	500	500	F	800	800	E	100p	100p	F	230p	230p	M	530p	530p	F	830p	830p	O
12	O	130	130	F	230	230	M	530	530	F	830	830	O	130p	130p	F	330p	330p	M	630p	630p	F	930p	930p	O
13	O	230	230	F	330	330	M	630	630	F	930	930	O	230p	230p	F	400p	400p	M	700p	700p	F	1000p	1000p	O
14	O	300	300	F	430	430	M	730	730	F	1030	1030	O	330p	330p	F	500p	500p	M	800p	800p	F	1100p	1100p	O
15	O	400	400	F	530	530	M	830	830	F	1130	1130	O	430p	430p	F	600p	600p	M	900p	900p	F			
16	O	500	500	F	630	630	M	930	930	F	1230	1230	O	530p	530p	F	630p	630p	M	930p	930p	F			
17	F	1230a	1230a	O	500	500	F	700	700	M	1000	1000	F	100p	100p	O	600p	600p	F	730p	730p	M			
18	F	130	130	O	630	630	F	800	800	M	1100	1100	F	200p	200p	O	700p	700p	F	830p	830p	M			
19	F	230	230	O	730	730	F	900	900	M	1200	1200	F	300p	300p	E	800p	800p	F	930p	930p	M			
20	M	1230a	1230a	F	330	330	O	830	830	F	1000	1000	M	100p	100p	F	400p	400p	E	900p	900p	F	1030p	1030p	M
21	M	130	130	F	430	430	O	930	930	F	1130	1130	M	230p	230p	F	530p	530p	E	1030p	1030p	F	1130p	1130p	M
22	M	230	230	F	530	530	O	1030	1030	F	1200	1200	M	300p	300p	F	600p	600p	E	1100p	1100p	F			
23	F	1230a	1230a	M	330	330	F	630	630	O	1130	1130	F	100p	100p	M	400p	400p	F	700p	700p	O			
24	F	130	130	M	430	430	F	730	730	O	1230	1230	F	200p	200p	M	500p	500p	F	800p	800p	O			
25	F	230	230	M	530	530	F	830	830	O	130p	130p	F	300p	300p	M	600p	600p	F	900p	900p	O			
26	F	300	300	M	600	600	F	900	900	E	200p	200p	F	330p	330p	M	630p	630p	F	930p	930p	O			
27	O	100	100	F	400	400	M	700	700	F	1000	1000	E	300p	300p	F	430p	430p	M	730p	730p	F	1030p	1030p	O
28	O	130	130	F	430	430	M	730	730	F	1030	1030	E	330p	330p	F	500p	500p	M	800p	800p	F	1100p	1100p	O
29	O	230	230	F	530	530	M	830	830	F	1130	1130	E	430p	430p	F	530p	530p	M	830p	830p	F	1130p	1130p	O
30	O	300	300	F	600	600	M	900	900	F	1200	1200	E	500p	500p	F	600p	600p	M	900p	900p	F			
31	O	500	500	F	630	630	M	930	930	F	1230	1230	E	530p	530p	F	630p	630p	M	930p	930p	F			

Locate the OPStime between the start and end times. For example on June 1, if you want to schedule your appointment in an Excellent Green time look for the E for Excellent Green times and you will notice that it falls between a start time of 5am and and end time of 1000am. Schedule your appointment accordingly.

O is Optimum Gold | E is Excellent Green | M is Moderate Blue | F is Fair Red | Add one hour for Daylight Savings Time to times shown.

INDEX OF CHARTS AND TABLES

Sample OPS Day 21
Taylor's Sample OPS Day 25-26
Activities that Should and Should Not be Scheduled During Optimum Gold 27
Activities that Should and Should Not be Scheduled During Excellent Green 27-28
Activities that Should and Should Not be Scheduled During Moderate Blue 28
Activities that Should and Should Not be Scheduled During Fair Red 29
Taylor Construction Company Percent of Appointments Sold for Robert S. 36
Taylor Construction Company Percentage of Appointments Sold 37
Planning Meeting Times According to Category of Meeting 40
OPS Activity Chart 48
OPS Best Strategy Chart 49
Average Number of Restaurant Customers Per Hour During Peak Meals 51
OPS Day for Bill Mink (Restaurant Manager) 52
Non-OPS Day for Diane Wilson (Director of Human Resources) 56-57
OPS Day for Diane Wilson 58-59
OPS Day for Lewis Kinney (Marketing Director for Construction/Leasing/Management Corporation) 71-72
Circadian Day for Spencer Lawson (Advertising Director) 74-75
Non-OPS Day for Sandra Myers (Account Representative for Public Relations Agency) 77-78
OPS Day for Sandra Myers 79-80
Percent Deviation of Births Occurring in Each OPS Time Relative to the Baseline Average of 11.96 Births Per Hour 87
OPS Day for Ken Weinberg (Senior Real Estate Investment Analyst) 109-110
Non-OPS Day for Todd Hastings (Second-Shift Quality Control Inspector) 114-115
OPS Day for Jannett Sibley (Singer/Songwriter) 117-118
Sample Pages from Executive OPStime Planner 122-123
Comparison of Percent of Day in Each OPS Time with Number of Accidents 130
The Optimum Performance Schedule for June 1994-June 1995 139-151

Get the Competitive Edge
ORDER YOUR OPS Executive Performance Package TODAY!

By now you are aware of the dramatic difference OPS can make in your life. To make it even easier for you, we have developed a Personal Performance Planner—the OPStimer 6-ring notebook in a handy travel size. It includes a 2-page-per-day OPS color calendar PLUS:

* Executive Personality Profile: Helps you increase your potential and maximize your results

* Introductory Cassette: Motivates you and reinforces the use of the OPStimer and its value

* OPS Tips Pamphlet: An easy "How-To" aid

* Quarterly Newsletter

* OPS Phone Support

In your OPS Executive Performance Package you will also receive:

* Map of U.S. with Time Zones and Area Codes
* Year-at-a-glance calendar
* 800 Travel Numbers
* Full-year monthly planning calendar
* Appointment, To-Do List, Mileage Record, Expenses
* Telephone and Address Directory
* Credit Card/Business Card holder and pocket

You will receive all this for $249 (plus $14.95 for shipping & handling).
Call 1-800-340-9009 for Corporate Pricing.

To order your OPS Executive Performance Package, please send the following coupon to:

Optimum Performance Technologies
P.O. Box 2164
Roswell, GA 30075

I am ordering (   ) (quantity) OPS Executive Performance Package(s) at the Introductory Price of $249 each PLUS $14.95 each for shipping and handling. (Georgia residents please add 6% state sales tax.)

NAME____
ADDRESS____
CITY____________________STATE___________ZIP___________
PHONE (   )_____________________________________

Check or money order enclosed.
OR YOU MAY ORDER BY CALLING 1-800-340-9009
Charge VISA MASTERCARD
Acct. #____________________Exp. Date_______________
Your Signature___________________________________

Please allow 4 to 6 weeks for delivery.